WAYNE'S WAR

WAYNE MYLES BURTON

To Mark

In peace we hope.

Wayne M Burton

Designed and produced by
Maine Authors Publishing
12 High Street, Thomaston, Maine
www.maineauthorspublishing.com

Printed in the United States of America

Elizabeth Morgan Burton

To my wife, Betsy, I'm very sorry for what I put you through and grateful for the crinkly, sweet smelling, sanity-saving letters I received from you almost daily. That the Army (apparently for intelligence reasons) made us burn all received correspondence before removing us from the Mekong Delta, leaves my daily letters to you, which you saved, as the sole source for our story. But they couldn't burn the memories of your loyal support throughout my tour nor what I know was a very hard time for you, also.

Map 1. 9th Infantry Division tactical area of responsibility, 31 August 1968

CONTENTS

PROLOGUE

The rising sun's shimmering waves bathing the Washington Mall in pastel pinks and oranges helped my mood little as I strode toward the Vietnam Veterans Memorial Wall on a long-delayed reunion with my past. In June 1999, three decades after leaving Vietnam, I had decided to visit this monument to futility and come to grips with my experience during the war our country would rather forget. My early-morning visit came in the middle of my trip to Nashville, Tennessee. There I would fulfill one month of the two-month residency obligation required by the Vanderbilt EdD program I had started the year before in their off-site program in New Hampshire.

As I walked among the memorials heading for mine, I couldn't help but notice that the wars we win get columns of names and music played by dancing fountains.

WW II Memorial, Washington, DC

For wars we lose, we get a diagonal trench symbolic of our uneasiness and unresolved conflict with regard to the Vietnam War's meaning. Nonetheless, there is power in the presentation of the names of the dead etched into the reflecting marble, allowing us to honor those who died for their country while dishonoring the war itself.

Vietnam Veterans Memorial Wall, Washington, DC

In the information next to the memorial, a directory of the names on the wall guides the visitor to the panel where they can find a particular name etched into the shiny marble surface. Through the directory, I found the name of Robert Boyd, a friend and member of my class of 1966 at Bowdoin College, where we had both joined ROTC. Bob, a warm, friendly person, blond and of slim build with a ready grin and very athletic, took the military training quite seriously, contemplating making the Army his career. I signed up to get the $40/month stipend to fund my social life and to get academic credit for the courses and help keep my flagging GPA above water.

Bob was killed just before he was to return home and marry his childhood sweetheart. He had served with great distinction in Vietnam and deserved the honors he received and the embrace of his family when he returned. At the base of the panel containing Bob's name, I placed one of the three Bronze Star ribbons I had been awarded during my tour.

As I sat on the grass banking opposite the panel with Bob's name, a small child walking by reached down to pick up the medal. His mother, a woman in her late twenties whose other hand he was clutching to balance himself, leaned down and gently told him to put it back. She explained with words to the effect that the medal must mean a lot to the person who had placed it there. She had no idea that that person was sitting less than six feet away, by then weeping uncontrollably.

The tears continued as I followed mother and son out of the trench, the slope up causing the number of names on successive panels to diminish until the list of the dead disappears when ground level is reached. I cried sporadically until I reached Nashville many hours later, my first post-traumatic stress episode—if that's what it was. Or it could have been simply profound sadness over the loss of Bob's promising life and the lives of the more than 58,000 others whose names populate the Memorial Wall.

I endured the long trip finding relief in the boxed Bruce Springsteen set, *Born in the USA* playing on the used blue Volvo's in-dash player. The interlude on one CD, in which he sits on the edge of the stage between songs telling the story of his pro-war father being initially angry when Bruce refused to enlist, got to me. I had to pull over, my vision impaired by tears. His dad had willingly answered the call when his country needed him in WW II. Bruce tells of getting his draft notice, and, in due course, reluctantly heads for his physical. Relieved when his flat feet exempt him from service, he doesn't look forward to his father's reaction when he learns his son can't fight.

Bruce chokes up reporting his surprise and gratitude when his father says "I'm glad" upon getting the news. Turns out the flood of body bags containing the remains of young men from "the hood" for a dubious purpose had caused his father to change his mind about the war. Bruce became an active war critic thereafter. From that point on, I gingerly began processing my Vietnam experience and the many questions I could not answer: How did I get there? What happened? And how has it affected the rest of my life?

While I came to oppose the war myself and wrote and spoke about it, I vowed to find answers to those more personal questions when I had more time. After reading my commanding general's obituary in the *Washington Post* in 1999 (which I reference in the chapters that follow), that smoldering ambition turned to flame when I retired from the presidency of North Shore Community College.

I finally approached and opened the several broken-down shoe boxes in our musty attic that contained the 240 letters I wrote my wife, Betsy, while I was in the Mekong Delta. She had saved them all. Hers to me had to be burned when my unit was redeployed from Vietnam. For this book, I decided to ground my Vietnam experience in those letters, adding my thoughts and embellishments almost a half century later. Perhaps my story can provide answers for others—former comrades under arms, surviving spouses and grandchildren, and members of subsequent generations contemplating both Vietnam and other undeclared wars.

Wayne Burton
June 2018

CHAPTER 1: CHICKEN WIRE

What it all boils down to is that I made the decision to go to Vietnam because this is where I feel I should try to use my abilities and feel I'm doing the right thing. In this I take some pride because now I can look at myself in the mirror and say, "Wayne, you're finally doing what you think you should be doing."

—Letter to my wife, December 12, 1968

Our boys in space are doing quite well—we can conquer space but can't end stupid conflicts like this one.

—Letter to my wife, July 18, 1969

I shook off the fog of a midafternoon nap on a cot outside my hot hooch in mid-July 1969 at Dong Tam, hoping that what they said was true: you don't hear the one that gets you. After another night of sleep-robbing enemy mortar and rocket attacks, the usual daytime lull provided welcome respite. Suddenly the distinctive *shush, shush, shush* of an enemy rocket-propelled grenade reached my ears just before the deadly oval with fins came into view cruising over the two-story building to my right. I rolled off the cot onto the ground, but my full-throated scream, "Incoming!" failed to reach many of the anxious soldiers in formation awaiting transport home fifty yards to my left.

A second later, the enemy's farewell message detonated in their midst, sending hot shrapnel into their bodies and shredding clothing, flesh, and bones of twenty-two of them. Rather than flying home to waiting loved ones, they would now wing to hospitals near Saigon or to US Navy ships offshore. Their cries for help brought several medics to stanch the wounds. Miraculously, none were killed on the spot, but I wondered if those badly wounded would make it.

If the round had landed a half football field shorter, I would have been one of those injured and might not be writing this. Then again, the sniper round that hit the sandbag a foot from my head a few nights before while on berm duty, or the rocket that landed on the jeep I had just jumped from for cover behind a blast wall a month ago, could have engraved my name with the 58,000 plus on Maya Lin's dark, below-grade Memorial Wall on the mall in Washington, DC.

Officers' quarters ("hooch"), Dong Tam, the 9th Infantry Division base camp on the banks of the Mekong River, Mekong Delta, South Vietnam

My name that July of 1969 identified a narrow-eyed cynic, a person much different from the wide-eyed idealist who'd arrived in Vietnam the previous December. Time in the steamy Mekong Delta had that effect.

We had departed Oakland, California, for Vietnam on Monday, December 16, 1968, at 9:30 a.m. on a sleek TWA 707 complete with attentive hostesses, nine channels in stereo, and a movie. I was still feeling the glow of our last night in the States. Four of us from the Boston area, having just endured our final "jungle fighting" training in the snowbanks of Fort Lewis, Washington, enjoyed our last supper at an upscale Seattle restaurant before heading for the war zone. I chose a filet of sole, a dish unlikely to be found in C-rations. At a table nearby, a graying husband and his lovely wife, both in their fifties and recently relocated from Boston, recognized our accent and asked us where we were from. Confirming that we were from the land without R's, they graciously invited us to their home for dessert and drinks. A nicer sendoff we could not have wished for.

The next morning, we were nervous but oddly relieved as we boarded the war-bound plane from Oakland. I took a last look back at mainland America and wondered if I would ever see it again.

I slept little on the overnight flight, and the next morning, I watched out the plane window as the island of Oahu came into view, our first stop before Vietnam. The left wing dipped and we nosed toward the airport in Honolulu.

After we landed, I wandered around the Honolulu Airport's tropical garden and contemplated the contents of the survival kits that had been handed to us as we embarked for the war zone. The packet included postcards, a toothbrush, toothpaste, soap, aspirin, and a small chess/checker set—for those idle moments in combat, I thought.

Our second stop for refueling and a new crew was Wake Island in the Philippines, famous for the gooney birds perched on the buildings by the runway. We had crossed the International Dateline and were magically forwarded into Tuesday. The smiling flight hostesses in their short dresses were replaced upon landing by fatigue-wearing GIs, their guttural "What do you wants" in sharp contrast to the musical "May I help yous" of the hostesses.

As the wheels lifted from the tarmac, the familiar theme song from *The Odd Couple* erupted out of the speakers while the small movie screen displayed Felix and Oscar arguing about household chores. The war and I would develop a similar relationship.

After a final stopover in Okinawa, we watched the end of *The Odd Couple* before landing at Bien Hoa Airbase in South Vietnam. I descended the stairs into what felt like a blast furnace, half expecting to see marching bands blaring patriotic songs while American flags flapped in the breeze to welcome us. But there was no band, no flags. Just GIs doing their jobs, seemingly indifferent soldiers loading the silver caskets of men whose time had been cut short into the hold of the plane for the trip home. Even in the oppressive heat, I shivered wondering if I, too, would return in the baggage hold someday.

We were driven from Bien Hoa to the depot at Long Binh where replacements were processed. The driver smirked a bit when I asked why the vehicle was wrapped in chicken wire. "Kids pull up beside us and throw hand grenades through the windows," he replied, checking out my new, not-yet-faded jungle fatigues and probably thinking I wouldn't last long in such ignorance. The wire did not prevent me from noting how small the people were and noticing the "abject squalor," as I wrote to Betsy, in which they lived. I had left her at my parents' house in Belmont, Massachusetts, where we'd said our good-byes. She had been too distraught to accompany me to Boston's Logan airport, from which I would depart for the West Coast. I felt emotionally empty as we parted on the porch; Betsy was confused and sad, the reality of the whole year we would be apart beginning to sink in.

That first night in Long Binh, as I crawled into my assigned bunk, I saw three little girls peering at me over the foot of the metal bed frame, their brown eyes shifting back and forth. They had been cleaning the floor before I arrived. On closer look, I discovered they weren't girls at all but women my mother's age and older, and none was taller than her at 5'1".

Over time, I learned not to be fooled by the small stature of Vietnamese women. What they lacked in stature they made up for with immense courage and endless resourcefulness. Many women led Viet Cong units during what they called "the American War." I also learned that they were made leaders because, having agonized through childbirth, they were better able to withstand the torture that the "puppets" (South Vietnamese Army interrogators) subjected them to when they were captured (Lady Borton, After Sorrow). I wrote to Betsy, "I'll let them have some further time before judging them." Already, the seeds of doubt were implanting in my psyche: something was not quite right about Vietnam or the war I had gotten myself into.

Along with the wire-wrapped bus, the tiny old women, and the scalding heat, my first impressions included the red clay that blanketed the ground, got under my nails, and clogged my nostrils. That first night,

I crawled under my mosquito netting sniffling from a lingering cold and feeling lonely and confused. None of this squared with the way I had envisioned my entry into war. The stories in the war comics I had devoured as a kid all began and ended in glory, not ignominy.

The next day, I got my hair cut and was given new insignia for my uniforms, including the 9th Infantry Division patch resembling a flower. The troops affectionately dubbed it the "flaming asshole," an example of the kind of humor that became a key survival tactic in the war zone.

My fifth letter to my wife continues our love story, one that flows through the more than 240 letters that I wrote to her while in Vietnam. It was this tenuous link to a caring person that sustained me when surrealism threatened my sanity. In that fifth letter, I confessed to her, "I think about you all the time and how one doesn't appreciate somebody until they're gone. Strangely, it doesn't make me sad; it makes me happy knowing I've got a good wife to go home to."

Knowing that someone back home was waiting was the one thing that kept many of us going during long nights huddled in bunkers under fire. As I found out when processing my men for compassionate leave, "Dear John" letters from wives and girlfriends threw even the toughest soldiers into black holes of depression. Unless the letters had a whiff of untruth, I routinely approved the leave. For my part, I had promised Betsy I would write every day, and I kept that promise hoping she would respond in kind, and she did. For that, more than anything else, I owe her my life.

I spent that first night in the officers' club, which had been decorated for Christmas. But the 95-degree heat and Vietnamese rock-and-roll band could not match the warmth of Christmas in the snow of New Hampshire where Betsy's mother lived, and we would make our permanent home. Whatever shreds of religious belief I had held onto since childhood were fading fast. I began believing that the benevolent God my parents had me worshiping would never countenance the carnage being inflicted on this tiny country or on ours in protecting it. My Easter experience three months later capped that process, snuffing out my religious faith completely.

My feelings of insignificance heightened when the guy who was supposed to wake me the next morning forgot to do so, and I missed my flight to the Mekong Delta and my new assignment to the 9th Infantry. So I wandered around Long Binh for another day. I had run out of money and had to borrow fifteen dollars from the Red Cross. The only good thing about my head cold and the stifling heat was that I had smoked just two cigarettes in my first four days away. Later I quit completely when I pulled berm duty and the flare of a cigarette could draw lethal sniper fire.

In my letter to Betsy, I had also described the Vietnamese cleaning women as good dressers. "They wear these real tight-topped dresses," I wrote, "with an ankle-length skirt and slits all the way up to their waists. Under this, they wear silk pants." To allay any fears about my fidelity, I added, "Don't worry about these girls—they turn me off. They all look greasy." I feel guilty for maligning the fastidious Vietnamese women for a selfish purpose.

I was finding it very difficult to hate the people we had been trained to kill. The military's dehumanizing process labeling the Vietnamese "gooks" and "slopes" was designed to free us from our better instincts so we could kill indiscriminately. But that ran up against my nature, which was to be friends with everyone. The process of confronting the sexism and racism I had acquired growing up in the '50s began in Vietnam and continues to this day.

I finally made it to my new unit the next day and was assigned to the 9th Signal Battalion to await further orders as to my job. While the training I had undergone in Signal School at Fort Gordon, Georgia, did include a short infantry component, my first assignment in Germany had been with a long-range communications battalion with no infantry training needed. Our mission there was to provide backup communications with the White House if secure land lines connecting NATO forces with commanders in Washington were unavailable. As a young first lieutenant at the time, I had served as company commander for a signal company.

A signal battalion within an infantry division, however, is much different. As my commanding officer described to the officers' wives in his welcoming letter, "We provide all the communications support within the division, to include radio, telephone, teletype, and other means." In such a supporting role, Signal officers were looked down upon by the infantry branch even though the US Army considered Signal a combat arm that "fought as infantry when required," according to our job descriptions.

Our men supported the infantry troops' tactical field communications equipment with larger interunit equipment on the 9th Division's base camp dubbed Dong Tam (Vietnamese for brotherhood). Dong Tam

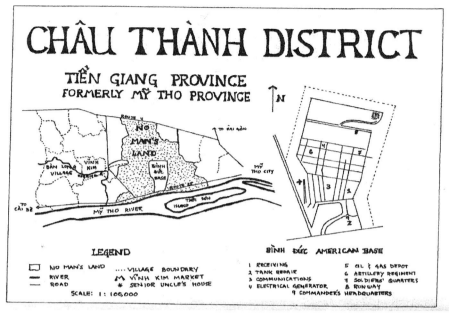

Map by Lady Borton, After Sorrow.
The Binh Duc Base at the left is the base's location.
The schematic on the right accurately shows detailed information.
My area, office, and hooch were in area 3

was an oval sprawl where my battalion was based, set within a one-mile perimeter on mud dredged up from the Mekong River by US Army Engineers. The base housed our artillery units, an airfield for helicopters and fixed-wing aircraft conducting air support operations, and the field hospital was next to our area. The base was protected by a berm, a buildup of mud and sand around the perimeter, into which we built fortified bunkers big enough to hold four or five men with slits facing outward and accommodating small arms as well as machine guns and other weaponry. The three-foot-thick sandbag walls protected fighters from shrapnel sprayed by enemy rocket and mortar fire. We installed overlapping rows of claymore mines in front of the berm, their green faceplates of serrated metal ready to shred intruders when we signaled through the wires stretching back into the bunker. Coils of razor wire wound beyond that.

In my new position as Adjutant or S1 of the 9th Signal Battalion, I was one of three captains serving on the battalion staff (S1: personnel, legal,

*Defensive bunker on the berm protecting
the 9th Infantry Division base camp at Dong Tam, 1969*

awards and decorations, other as required; S2/3: intelligence and operations; and S4: logistics and supplies). I was also assigned as the Headquarters Company Commander responsible for troops working in and around our headquarters and for ensuring that the dozen or so defensive positions on the berm were manned 24 hours a day, seven days a week.

It seemed odd that Signal Branch soldiers would pull such duty, as we were not trained for infantry work. The closest I had come to any such training had occurred in ROTC summer camp three years before. Until I recently read *The 9th Infantry Division in Vietnam: Unparalleled and Unequaled* by Major General Ira A. Hunt Jr. (The University Press of Kentucky, 2010), I did not realize why supporting Signal Branch troops would be pressed into infantry roles. He writes that to maximize the number of troops in the field, "the support troops took over from the combat units all the responsibilities for the Dong Tam perimeter defenses" (p. 25). With all of two weeks of infantry training in ROTC summer camp, I held responsibility for an active perimeter defense, land mines, machine guns, and field of fire coordination. That the Viet Cong never breached my sector is a miracle and a tribute to our noncommissioned officers and my men, who learned along with me. Just being on the base, of course, subjected us to assaults on the compound itself.

In his book, General Hunt also explains why Dong Tam, a formidable division headquarters base camp, came under attack so often. The Viet Cong and North Vietnamese Army units (NVA) who surrounded our base sought to reach and overrun Saigon to our north by launching a major assault through the Mekong Delta from the south. Thus, their main targets were regional capitals, Tan An and Ben Tre, where many US troops were deployed and several larger military installations, "particularly Dong Tam and the 7th ARVN Division headquarters in My Tho," were located. As one who traveled the road between Dong Tam and My Tho to oversee the orphanage we ran and to serve as a liaison to the 7th ARVN Division headquartered there, I can attest to the enemy presence along the route.

An Army of the Republic of South Vietnam bunker
provided security on the road connecting Dong Tam and My Tho City

Before I could begin my new job, I had to attend a rather worthless orientation on our base in Vietnam, much of which I'd already had at Fort Lewis, Washington, just before I left. My CO pulled me out early when I reported this to him. The only memorable component of the training session was watching an actual mission begin. In the field next to us, an American assault force jumped into helicopters to be flown to a target somewhere in our area. The soldiers looked younger than me and bore little resemblance to the hardened, bearded warriors my war comics had ingrained in my mind. Many lacked any beard at all. Much later, I learned that the average age of an American soldier in Vietnam was in the high teens, old enough to fight and die but not old enough to drink or vote. As the "eagle flight" of UH-1 choppers loaded with troops ascended into the sky and headed west, our trainers detected a VC unit close by and pulled us back inside the berm. Butterflies roiled in my stomach as I realized how close I was to real combat. This was no safe football scrimmage. This was for real.

My fear of being wounded or killed was compounded by my terror of being captured and tortured. During my training in ROTC summer camp, I had been subjected to Code of Conduct training to prepare me for the possibility of capture. In the next chapter I describe that ordeal and its effect on me.

In that day's letter to Betsy, I wrote that the sirens had gone off, signaling that incoming mortars were landing on our base. I was scared. Over the course of my tour, we experienced about 200 "red alerts," as they were called, some short-lived with only twenty or so rounds hitting. Others were much larger and longer, occasionally including a "ground probe" of enemy forces attempting to breach our fortifications. Each assault killed or wounded soldiers on the base and destroyed buildings and equipment. That first assault, on my first day in Dong Tam, began at 4:30 a.m. and lasted over an hour. Sleep deprivation became a way of life. Like all GIs, I slept as much as I could. But our twelve-hour workdays, seven days a week with assaults at night made for bleary eyes and frayed nerves, just what the enemy intended.

When the shrieking siren went off, our procedure was to run to the nearest fortified bunker. That first night, one of my sergeants taught me the key to survival—learning the difference between *boom-shish*, our own outgoing artillery fire, and *shish-boom*, incoming enemy mortars and rockets. Soon I didn't need the siren; I could tell the difference on hearing that sound, a skill that saved my life a few times.

The night before Christmas, six days after I arrived, Red Cross girls wearing Santa costumes were driven around the base singing carols. We watched movies on a barge in the river and followed up with several beers in our illegal officers' club, a living room–sized bar taking up two rooms in our BOQ—the bachelor officer quarters. This two-story rectangular building, subdivided into about twelve bedrooms we called our "hooches," was surrounded by sandbag blast walls six feet high and three feet thick. I came to appreciate having a room on the bottom floor after I learned that sniper fire from outside the base often hit the second-floor walls above me.

Our living conditions were spartan, with outhouses and cold showers the norm—when they were working. In my pre-Christmas letter to Betsy, I had included a list of things I needed, including more underwear, a pair of Bermuda shorts, a polo shirt, a fan, and shower clogs.

Orientation leaders had warned us of cultural differences that we had to respect. For example, when Vietnamese men walk together holding hands, it indicates friendship, not homosexuality. Pointing at a person to get their attention is considered insulting; that's how they call their animals. Because they believe that the head is sacred, it is a sacrilege to pat or touch somebody there, especially children. This would become important in my work with the orphanage.

Somewhere during my first days in country, I realized that the army career I had briefly flirted with was not for me. I had responded poorly to regimentation in my formative years, sometimes to my detriment. But my addiction to glory, which I'd achieved mostly through sports and false toughness, had me sacrificing my resistance to authority to gain public adulation. Growing up in a downscale double-decker in an upscale, single-family-house suburb of Boston, I had felt the sting of disrespect accorded the less wealthy families. In search of recognition, I worked hard at football and achieved a measure of fame. But that lasted only as long as the football season and graduation....

I glanced up at the large clock at the end of the field ticking off the last minutes of my college football career that chilly October day in the fall of 1965. The score on the board next to the clock did not matter. Several pads protecting my right arm did not protect me from the severe pain in that arm, which had been badly injured four games ago. My misaimed forearm had caught the face mask of the brute charging me, and the resulting ruptured veins and capillaries above my right elbow had turned my arm into a giant purple sausage.

But I was playing for the undermanned Bowdoin team, thinking the pain was worth the glory. My coach had switched me to right end from the left side so I could hit with my left arm while the right hung limply at my side sending shards of pain through me when it was moved at all. The stands that had never been full were emptying quickly, as the half-drunks headed to the fraternity houses, bored with our sacrifices on the gridiron. The glory of old was a thing of the past it seemed. In high school and earlier at Bowdoin, I had tasted the nectar of athletic success, the misty-eyed adoration of our fans for winning the state championship against all odds addicting me to acclaim. Much like heroin addicts getting their first fix, I wanted more. But my football career was fading fast and would end in 12:22. I needed a new drug.

The thrill of being saluted and called "sir" as commander-for-the-day of my ROTC battalion during drill three days prior had provided a welcome rush—not like a horse hit, but enough to give me a pleasant sensation. Hope raised its blemished head.

Before I volunteered for Vietnam, I had spent two years in Germany serving in a component of allied forces seeking to halt the advance of totalitarianism. I had felt a sense of honor that was reflected in the culture of the units we led and our own behavior. In Vietnam, our conflicting missions—winning the hearts and minds of the people with bullets and bombs—troubled me. In civilian life, at least I could pick my challenges. In the military, my battles would be picked for me.

After limited research, I had decided an MBA would give me the best opportunities in the civilian world. Thus, in the 100-degree heat, covered with red dust and scrambling to survive random mortar attacks, I launched my graduate education. I spent Christmas Eve 1968 studying for the Graduate Business Admissions test I hoped to take at the University of Maryland testing center in Saigon in early spring as part of my application to graduate school. With my mother-in-law in declining mental health, I knew it would be best to live somewhere near her, so I picked the University of New Hampshire for my master's degree.

On Christmas day 1968, we had a party for the officers at our little club. I wrote Betsy that night how everyone pretended to be having a good time, but we all suffered from homesickness. Our gift from the army was a Bob Hope show at Dong Tam with "Ann Margaret and all the girls."

At 6:00 a.m. on the morning of the big show, I marched a platoon of infantry into the arena fabricated for the event to reserve seats for our troops. Even though the show was not scheduled until 1:00 in the afternoon, we were not taking any chances about getting good seats. The show "wasn't bad," I reported to Betsy, except for the huge scaffolding for the cameras and other TV production equipment that limited the view of the stage for many at ground level. So much for reserving good seats.

Hope told a few raunchy jokes and the fourteen-member Gold Diggers danced and pranced to the delight of the several thousand troops. Our commanding officer, General Julian Ewell, failed miserably at trying to be funny. The show ended with a bang. Our batteries of 155mm artillery let loose a salvo as part of a fire mission called in from a combat unit operating in our area. After the short time I had been in country, I was already used to the round-the-clock shelling of targets unknown. But the booming artillery assailing our ears and vibrating the ground unraveled Bob Hope and his flock. They hustled to their waiting Chinook helicopters and departed in a cloud of dust for safer climes.

Though cut short by the artillery fire, the show itself was a success for the craven GIs. The division's combat photographers had infiltrated the Gold Diggers changing area and published a scrapbook of their handiwork. They technically reported to me, though I cannot say I directed their work in this or any other instance. I do recall that of the dozen or so reporting to me, over half were killed in combat. To record the action, they placed themselves in harm's way and paid the ultimate price for their work.

If asked to reduce my Vietnam experience to a one-word answer, my best is "surreal," meaning "unexpected juxtapositions," according to Random House. In the case of the Hope CSO Christmas show, a modern comedy hour staged amidst artillery shells firing at suspected hostile targets nearby fits that definition.

In 1996, during an event featuring Senator John Kerry, I mentioned in our conversation that, like him, I am a Vietnam vet. He asked me where I served, and I told him in the Mekong Delta. He raised his eyebrows and

*Ninth Division troops crane their necks
to see Bob Hope and company's performance, December 1968*

*Then Senator John Kerry and the author
swap stories about the Hope concert in 1996*

said, "So did I." His curiosity piqued, he asked, "When did you serve there?" and I said in 1968 and 1969. Looking really shocked, he tilted his head and said, "Where were you?" My answer, Dong Tam, almost brought him to his knees as he chuckled, "That's where I was!"

He then asked if I remembered the Bob Hope show of December 1968. When I nodded, he told me his experience with that event. Having heard about the show when downriver, he informed his crew that he was heading back to Dong Tam to catch Bob Hope and his troupe. Somehow, he took a bad right turn into a canal that ran beside Dong Tam that we had dubbed the "VC Canal" due to the significant number of enemy soldiers clustered there. Kerry's Swift boat was barely able to turn around in the narrow steam and escape the enemy fire that came from both sides. By the time he got to the site of the show, Hope had already packed up and left, much to Kerry and his crew's chagrin.

"The waterway suddenly took on a very hostile aspect," Kerry said. So he decided, with little discussion, to turn around and head back downriver. PCF-44 headed at full speed out of the canal, which could not have been more than 60 feet wide (Douglas Brinkley, *Tour of Duty*, p. 224–225; HarperCollins, 2004). When the Swift finally made it back to the My Tho River, the show was over. "The visions of Ann Margaret and Miss America and all the other titillating personalities who would have made us feel so at home hung around us for a while until we saw the three Chinook helicopters take off from the field and presumed that our dreams had gone with them. We had stupidly taken one of the most notorious Viet Cong–infested waterways in the vicinity searching naively for Bob Hope," Kerry wrote in his notebook. "It simply hadn't occurred to us that Bob Hope did not change the status of the war. The VC still existed."

Our connection and friendship continued after that as he considered me an unofficial member of his Band of Brothers. In 2004, I served as a delegate to the Democratic National Convention when he ran for president, and he invited me to meet him at the Boston Naval shipyard when he arrived. Prior to that, I had spent time with his crew and with Jim Rassman, the Green Beret Kerry had pulled from a river, exposing himself to enemy fire to save the wounded man's life. Both his men and Rassman praised both Kerry's courage and his devotion to his men. That he was wounded three times and, in accordance with policy was sent home early, speaks to his extraordinary service.

Following the convention in 2004, however, his opponent tried to turn this favorable narrative into a negative. At that point, I gladly served as a damage-control person responding to the unfair media assaults on Kerry that followed.

*The author greets Kerry as he arrives
for the 2004 Democratic National Convention*

Many other events contributed to the cognitive dissonance that afflicted so many soldiers then and to this day, perhaps accounting for the high suicide rates among Vietnam veterans. It began with our mission: to win the hearts and minds of the populace, an endeavor otherwise known as "pacification," while killing as many suspected Viet Cong as possible. Accomplishing that mission without significant collateral killing of innocent civilians, the ones whose hearts and minds we were trying to win over, proved impossible.

In his book, General Hunt touts the accomplishments of the division I served in. But he also acknowledges that "With such intense operations, civilian casualties sometimes occurred." When "injuries came to our attention, solatium was instantly offered." I was, in fact, given a "Solatium Payment" book indicating how much we should pay survivors for a lost limb or a dead child or other relative. As our battalion's designated Civic Action Officer, I did travel to villages in which victims were due solatium payments. Once again, the surreal nature of paying for the human damage we wrought depressed me deeply, so much so that I delegated that duty to another officer to avoid the pain and contempt in the payees' eyes.

While the 9th Infantry Division received the highest number of unit awards for its performance in Vietnam, it came with a cost the extent of which I did not realize until 2009, when I read the obituary of our CO, General Julian Ewell. Operation Speedy Express had wreaked havoc on the Mekong Delta civilians. Back then, as the list of solatium payments grew long, I had begun to wonder why so many civilians were being injured or killed if, as I assumed, precautions were being taken to minimize civilian casualties. The daily intelligence reports I saw had included the number of enemy and Americans killed and wounded the previous day. No mention was made of civilian casualties, so I assumed, since I knew they were occurring, that the number was probably included in the enemy killed count.

"If a gunner saw anyone," a Vietnamese farmer who survived the conflict told Lady Borton during an interview for her book, *After Sorrow: An American Among the Vietnamese*, "even a woman or a small child or a water buffalo, he blew them apart. Once, there was a woman in Cai Lay district. They shot off her arm, so it dangled. Her husband had to cut off the rest. She had children. They might as well have killed her." (*After Sorrow*: 1995, Viking Penguin Books)

The hundreds of tranquil hamlets were suspect and subjected to harsh treatment because they furnished "sustenance and manpower to the VC units." General Hunt concedes that "it was often extremely difficult to differentiate friends from foe; there was always an opportunity for collateral damage." I liken it to being asked to enter an American town and eliminate all Democrats or Republicans. Might as well eliminate the whole town.

In his epic film for the Public Broadcasting System, *The Vietnam War* (2016), Ken Burns includes an interview with Colonel Robert Gard, an artillery commander with the 9th Division when I was there who asserts it "defies imagination" that a kill ratio of 45:1, Vietnamese to Americans killed, would not include noncombatants. Our commanding officer, General Julian Ewell, according to the Burns film, publicly declared "that the hearts and minds approach can be overdone. In the Delta, the only way to overcome VC control and terror is through brute force."

Under Ewell's Free Fire Zone concept, anyone out after the dusk curfew should be shot. During the day, anyone seen running should be targeted. We followed his orders in the field and from the bunkers I controlled on our perimeter.

Settling into my new life was facilitated greatly by the camaraderie among the captains and lieutenants in my battalion. Most of us were just out of college and at age 24, like me, held the lives of several hundred men in their hands. We had to grow up fast. A new friend with whom I became very close during my tour was the man whose position I took. "The guy I'm replacing is a colored guy named Jim Coleman," I wrote to Betsy in my letter of December 26th. "I've become very good friends with him, so the transition won't be too hard." Jim, who was considering an army career, had been appointed a line company commander. More on him later.

I also began collecting dogs for companionship. I wrote Betsy, "There's a dog I named Bruno who likes to sleep under my desk. He's a mutt that looks like a husky and hates Vietnamese. Every time one of the Vietnamese cleaning women go by, he goes after her. Therefore, he's a great watchdog."

Tender moments were hard to come by in Vietnam, but one happened the night of December 26, 1968, at that month's Hail and Farewell, a traditional military event where departing friends are honored and new officers are welcomed. I wrote to Betsy, "Tonight at the Hail & Farewell we had some punch in small silver cups and our CO proposed a toast to our wives. We all toasted and a quiet came over the room. Wives are a very revered thing over here. Especially you, dear."

CHAPTER 2: TORTURE, AMERICAN STYLE

The routine march back to our barracks after a day of training on the Code of Conduct and Escape and Evasion at Fort Devens, Massachusetts, in the summer of 1966 took an unexpected harsh turn for my company of ROTC cadets. Having just completed simulated patrols through a mock Vietnam village, we were suddenly captured by realistic-looking Viet Cong.

They marched us into a simulated Viet Cong encampment complete with bonfires and ropes hanging from trees, some hoisting cadets off the ground screaming in pain from the electricity coursing through their bodies.

Three burly "VC" tied rope wrapped around a tree limb to my wrists and pulled me off the ground yelling questions in my face. "How many men in your unit?" "What's your mission?" "Who's your company commander?" When I refused to disclose anything but my name, rank, and serial number, as directed during the morning lectures, the lead interrogator ordered the man kneeling behind me to "wire him up."

As a weightlifting former pulling guard on the Bowdoin football team who rarely missed a play due to injury and was known for high pain tolerance, the bolt of electricity from the wires on my legs sent excruciating pain shooting through my body like shards of broken glass. The screaming intensified around me, and suddenly I realized it was me. My legs jumped uncontrollably for what seemed like a lifetime but was half a minute or so.

The interrogator fired more questions at me, and I yelled my name, rank, and serial number at him, and I recall trying to kick him in the face as my legs swung below me. Fear began crawling up my back as I realized my captors had no use for the Geneva Convention. The interrogator instructed his helper to increase the voltage and make it last longer. The second jolt made my legs dance even faster, and I screamed in pain again but recall trying to spit at the interrogator, the saliva pouring from my mouth my only weapon.

They gave me one more charge when I stuck to name, rank, and serial number, and I think I passed out. I came to on the floor of a hut with other captives. A trapdoor in the floor opened over a river, and as we'd been trained, we jumped in and swam downstream looking for the "friendly farmer" we'd been instructed to find. Soaked and chagrined, we struggled from the water into the hut on the riverbank with the light hanging outside and waited for the deuce-and-a-half to mercifully pick us up and take us to our barracks.

The pain of torture seared my memory such that I always carried a loaded .45 in Vietnam, in addition to my M-16, to use on myself if I were ever close to being captured. The cadets rarely talked about our experience. I still do not. No one wants to remember pain. But it was also the humiliation of being violated in such a way that kept our experience buried.

At least one of my fellow cadets broke under the electric shock and was subjected to more torture as he spilled his life story or anything the torturers asked for. Another cadet never returned to complete his training, as I recall.

A Google search confirmed that such a training center had been built at Ft. Devens in the '60s to prepare trainees for the Vietnam War. The Tactical Training Center (TTC), as it was named, was the brainchild of Lt. Col. Lewis Millett, a Korean War Medal of Honor winner who sought to provide as realistic a replication of the conditions in Vietnam as he could. "He found Vietnamese-speaking soldiers or Asian-Americans to play the roles of Viet Cong aggressors."

As it's described in a press story, "Not all students were successful in making their way back to friendly lines, and some were captured by Viet Cong patrols. Those students underwent simulated but surprisingly harsh interrogation. The simulated capture and interrogation gave the soldiers an opportunity to practice and apply the Code of Conduct. After 15 to 20 minutes of interrogation, the students could escape and rejoin their comrades."

The exercise may have been simulated, but the electricity that caused every fiber in my body to feel like it was on fire was all too real. For the rest of my life, when I hear of torture, I shudder with the memory of that night of terror at the hands of my own country.

CHAPTER 3: RACE

"They always sent the black soldiers in first to trigger our traps."
—*Second Harvest (pseudonym), a former Viet Cong leader,
commenting on American tactics for Lady Borton's* After Sorrow

Having grown up in Belmont, a nearly all-white suburb of Boston, I had never known anyone who wasn't white. My parents had been active members of a Congregational church in our town. My father served as deacon and directed the Sunday School, and my mother, an accomplished pianist, directed the church choirs. Against their wishes, my sister and I fell away from organized religion in our early teens. While they reluctantly accepted our Catholic friends, they prohibited us from entering a Catholic church. My inviting a Jewish girl to the junior high prom angered them, but they allowed it. My date's parents unsuccessfully tried to stop her, too. Neither she nor I understood their ire.

My parents were not racist in the angry, hating sense. But they were biased, both products of Yankee forebears, who skirted the race issue when it was raised in our household. They were not apt to rent to blacks or Asians the two apartments that were part of the twin two-family homes where my parents and my grandparents, who owned the two double-deckers, each occupied one unit.

At Bowdoin, my undergraduate college, minority students were rare. The only black member of my class (1966), had grown up in Boston and likely found the environment in Brunswick, Maine, less than friendly. Certainly it was that way on campus. My fraternity, Kappa Sigma, belonged to a national organization that prohibited pledging Jews or African-Americans. Despite the prohibition, we did have several Jewish members, but we did not invite the black student to any pledging events even though he had become friends with me and others by being on the football team. While Jewish members blended with the white members, to keep our charter, our leadership sought to avoid obvious conflicts with the national fraternity's rules.

Eventually, one of the independent fraternities with many Jewish members did pledge the black student. He graduated with our class, eventually got his PhD, and taught philosophy at a university in the South. But his being black-balled by the Kappa Sigma national organization bothered me and others in my fraternity. I supported our move to leave the national organization in protest when they caught us discussing the issue with other chapters, and in my junior year, they threatened to expel us from the national organization. I wish I could say that I was a leader in the effort for change. But, being more taken with partying and football, I was not paying attention to moral issues. Several alumni expressed anger over Kappa Sigma "going local," but we persisted, and the fraternity lived on as independent Alpha Kappa Sigma.

In the mid-'90s, Bowdoin no longer recognized any organization that discriminated, a step I strongly supported. Today the site of the former Alpha Kappa Sigma sports the college's newly opened Roux Center for the Environment.

Our rebellion against our national fraternity flared into action in part because the civil rights movement touched Bowdoin in the spring of 1964. One night, my roommate, Leo, whose parents both practiced law, looked up from his constitutional law text and eyeballed me doodling in my economics workbook and silently debating whether to continue studying or join other friends for beers downtown. When I asked Leo his plans, I expected his response to be that we go downtown and meet up with them. Instead, he invited me to go with him to hear a guest speaker in the Moulton Union across the quad.

"This is a very special speaker," Leo said, his tone serious.

The invitation turned out to be life-changing for me.

The elegant Reading Room in the Moulton Union, trimmed with shiny dark oak and carpeted with Orientals, filled quickly with Bowdoin students, faculty, and staff, along with townspeople, all there to hear the speaker, Dr. Martin Luther King Jr., advocate for the voting rights legislation pending in Congress.

He sat in a large chair like a throne at the right side of the rectangular room. Six large black men flanked him, three on each side, their backs against the wall, their eyes darting around the room looking for any-one who might be hiding a weapon. The threats on Dr. King's life had increased exponentially as the civil rights movement gained traction.

Dressed in a black suit and red tie, he spoke with the eloquence of the minister he was and the knowledge of our political system that he had mastered. His powerful dignity quieted the room as he began his presentation chronicling the history of the civil rights movement. His deep voice rose as he expounded on the importance of extending voting rights to all, a key to the movement's success.

Later that evening, Dr. King informally met with me and a few other interested students over coffee in the cafeteria in the Moulton Union opposite where he had spoken the night before. Our conversation ranged widely, and at one point, I recall telling him how taken I was with his message. What I sought to understand, however, is what it had to do with me, a white guy on an all-white campus in a mostly all-white state.

On May 6, 1964, Dr. Martin Luther King Jr. came to Bowdoin College to speak about the civil rights movement and the importance of ending segregation and discrimination in America.

"If democracy is to live, then segregation must die. Segregation is a cancer in the body politic..." *Martin Luther King Jr.*

Dr. Martin Luther King Jr. at Bowdoin College, May 6, 1964.

Extracted from Bowdoin Magazine, *January 19, 2009*

He leaned forward, fixing me in his gaze, both arms folded on the table. "If your conscience stops at the border of Maine," he warned, "you're less of a person than you should be. You are as responsible for what happens in Birmingham as you are in Brunswick."

I can't say I became an instant activist, but he was the first to challenge me to expand my conscience. I had pulled back from a newfound idealism following the assassination of President John F. Kennedy the year before, though his *ask not...* directive had stuck in my head. I promised Dr. King I would help him achieve his dream, not knowing I was speaking to a young man whose life would change the world less than four years after his night in Brunswick.

Our paths crossed again four years later in a way we could not have anticipated. I had graduated from college, been commissioned as a second lieutenant in the US Army Signal Corps, and been assigned to a base in Europe. Southern Germany in early April had not warmed enough to go without a field jacket. I ventured outside the guard shack where I was serving as Duty Officer for Nureut Kaserne, an American base near Karlsruhe on the Swiss border. The date was April 4, 1968.

The radio crackled then sputtered as someone obviously in peril yelled, "There's a riot at the EM Club! Get the OD [Duty Officer] down here fast. They're destroying the place!"

A chill went up my spine, as I had expected the usual quiet night commanding the small Unit Police (UP) force detailed to base security. But already I could hear the noise from the riot.

I and a small crew of "Keystone Cops" jumped into a revving jeep and headed toward the Enlisted Men's Club a few blocks away. At that point, we had no clue what was causing the disturbance.

On the way, I checked my .45, filling the cavity in the handle with a full clip. It contained a dozen rounds. I asked myself if I should wait for the real MPs to arrive, but my football instincts kicked in and we kept going.

En route, I learned that at 6:05 p.m. US time, 9:05 German time, a sniper's bullet had shattered the skull of Dr. Martin Luther King Jr., killing him on the balcony of the Lorraine Motel in Memphis, Tennessee.

He had been the one great hope for change embraced by blacks across the US and on military bases all over the world. Our black troops, inflamed with anger and outrage, took their frustrations out on the furnishings of their club, just as mobs rioted in New York, Chicago, Los Angeles, and other urban centers.

I jumped from the jeep along with my men and waded into the screaming mob. I pulled out my .45, intending to fire warning shots, when a stocky buck sergeant I recognized from the motor pool emerged from the melee. He had a knife in his hand and stuck it so close to my throat I could make out the barbs on the top used for fileting.

By instinct, I stuck my .45 in his chest and our eyes locked. We had always gotten along, but now I could see in his eyes the hatred for the race I represented. We had stolen his spiritual and political leader. We had destroyed the man who sought to free millions from the bonds of second-class citizenship, legal disenfranchisement, limited educational opportunities, and other indignities.

I wondered if I could kill him before he plunged the knife into my throat. He blinked when I pulled the slide back to chamber a round. He waivered as my eyes changed from fearsome intensity to deep sympathy. He lowered the knife and I lowered my pistol. He did not resist as the sergeant with me twisted his arms behind his back, clicked on the handcuffs, and turned him toward the jeep. He was taken to the MP station and ultimately to the military jail in Heidelberg, just north of us. Shortly after that, our Military Police arrived in force, some black themselves, and quelled the rioting.

I later found out my assailant had pled guilty to assaulting an officer and had been busted two grades and fined but not jailed, much to my relief. He could not have known that Dr. King and I had a history between us and that his death had devastated me also.

The process of overcoming my own racism was now well under way. Dr. King's death began to give me a new appreciation for what the world looked like through the eyes of those facing institutional and personal racism, something I had never fully appreciated growing up white.

My education on racial matters accelerated when Captain James E. Coleman, the person I replaced as Adjutant of the 9th Signal Battalion, 9th Infantry Division in Vietnam, promised to take time to train me on my new responsibilities, a commitment he kept. I will be forever grateful to him for bringing me up to speed in a brand-new job in which competence saved lives. The tall, slim man with a slightly twisting walk and a sardonic expression chuckled much, seeing humor in our lives that made our situation livable. But underneath, I knew a sadness lay close to the surface about the tendency of others to underrate him because of his race, a feature of racism from which we all suffered negative consequences.

He also educated me on what growing up black was like, a perspective that has informed me ever since. But I had a long road to travel in this respect and wrote that to Betsy in my letter of January 6, 1968, about the man who became my best friend in Vietnam.

...Jim Coleman, a Negro captain whose job I took and who is now a CO. He still has all the same mannerisms and does not try to talk like a white guy. He's funny, and we talk a lot about different things. Jim's problem is he's hard to work for. He knows how things should be done and can't adjust to different circumstances. He does not have many friends here except for me because I do understand his problem. Of course, being the only colored officer is a little tough, too. He never talks about his color like some I know and just wants to be respected for what he is. For this I respect him. He's a college grad and has a beautiful wife named Viola. He has one son who is a big fella. Pictures of his family adorn all his walls, and whenever I go in his hooch, I say hello to Viola and he chuckles about it.

Captains Wayne Burton, Ron Griese, and James Coleman in formation during a command ceremony on Dong Tam, South Vietnam, May 1969

Racial tension boiled under the surface in Vietnam. Interdependence held it down, at least in our unit. In other units, rumors circulated of "fragging"—the wounding and sometimes killing of noncommissioned officers and commissioned officers by their own men. The violence was not necessarily driven by racism as much as by animosity toward higher-ranking people. But race was a factor.

Our commanding officer once expressed concern over a black insurrection that he felt was coming, and he wanted to take steps to stop it. The responsibility for dealing with this possibility fell on Jim Coleman because he was black and on me because I was Jim's friend and the battalion's chief personnel officer. Jim rightly resented that task. I agreed with him that racism was a primarily white affliction that blacks should not have to rectify.

Jim and I conversed frequently about the subject, especially as he dealt with white officers who found him suspect due to his race and black soldiers who accused him of being an "Oreo"—black on the outside but white on the inside. I described one such conversation to Betsy in my letter of January 28, 1969.

Last night as I was going back to my hooch, I ran into my friend Jim Coleman. He invited me to the lounge for a few beers because it was his third wedding anniversary. He's spent a year and a half of it in Vietnam. Anyway, we got talking about the race problems. He grew up in the slums of Baltimore and worked his way through college. He told me some experiences he's had that would make your hair curl.

Anyway, he doesn't hate white people but just doesn't understand why they [blacks] are all classed as niggers when he's as smart as any of them. He can't walk through certain sections of towns, his wife is exiled from the Officers' Wives Club, nobody came to visit them, and he knows he's going to have a tougher time than if he were white. And he doesn't appreciate the Negro jokes some people tell him just to prove they are not prejudiced. I admire him, dear, because he will have it tough, and he doesn't deserve that just because his skin is black. Now don't be thinking I'm flying off on a crusade or something because I'm not. A majority or so of colored people are a little different and can't be trusted. Anyway, Jim and I discussed it until 2:30 a.m. and of course could not come to any real conclusions.

The only thing we did conclude was that until the white community stops feeling proud because they give the Negro a little bit, and until whites grow up and realize that the reason blacks are different is because they have never been given a chance, there won't be peace. By the same token, until blacks realize that they are not different and that they must understand the white position, they're not going to get ahead. Jim's sort of a militant because he can't see any other way to fight back and, in a way, he's right. He says he's better off in Vietnam because he can't stand turning the other cheek when he can't get served in a restaurant or get a decent apartment. Believe me, it was an objective discussion, and I think I learned something from him. We were completely candid as I told him black people make me nervous.

It was rather humorous, too, because he never saw his first white man chewing gum until he was 17. You see, in the school he went to the teachers (all black) always used whites to set the example. In other words, his teacher would say, "Don't chew gum, Jimmy; the white kids don't do that." And when he was 17, he saw some white kids chewing gum and was flabbergasted. He takes his showers late at night because people stare at him. He's not imagining it, either….The conversation was basic and philosophical, and I learned something from him. One shouldn't make judgments until one has seen both sides or lived both sides as was the case here—end of proverb of the day.

What I did not tell Betsy was the circumstance that had led Jim to be in Vietnam for his second tour. After the first tour, he was stationed at a base in the South where his wife was treated badly. At that point, he had planned on making the army his career, so he volunteered to do a second combat tour so his wife would not have to live near the base that he was assigned to in Georgia. He would not tolerate the "Whites Only" signs found in that region during that time. While he was in Vietnam, she could live near their families around Baltimore.

The strategy to stifle racial unrest took several forms, including, I sensed, prosecuting black soldiers more strenuously than whites. I shall never erase from my mind the image of a black enlisted man facing an all-white special court-martial in an underground, candlelit bunker more suitable for a KKK meeting than for meting out impartial justice. I believe the charge was possession of marijuana, for which most any GI could be arrested, but blacks were targeted disproportionately. He was sentenced to the in-country jail, busted in rank, and no doubt received a bad conduct discharge that would hamper him all his life.

He had no lawyer to advise him because under the misnamed Uniform Code of Military Justice, military law at the time, none was required. A young lieutenant would "defend" him from a script that I, as the unit's legal officer, prepared. What he was not advised about was that the court itself was illegal. The UCMJ required that a special court-martial be comprised of officers from outside the unit of the accused. That was never the case in our unit, and I was reprimanded when I raised the issue.

On one occasion, during a writer's workshop, we were asked to write a dialogue through the eyes of another person. I seized on the challenge of writing my recollection of a meeting we'd once had, called by our CO to discuss black unrest and possible fragging in our unit. What follows is that piece, which is grounded in my general memory of the meeting with dialogue written through the eyes of my friend, Captain Coleman.

"I'm concerned the unrest among Negroes in the battalions will spread to others including whites, and we need to act, now!" the colonel barked, looking each of us in the eye in turn. "Reports of men disobeying direct orders reach me daily, and I want something done about that. What's wrong with these people?" he queried looking me in the eye for the second time.

These people, I thought. You mean me, don't you, colonel, the only Negro in the room. I was acutely aware of the rumblings among the black troops who comprised almost half of our battalion. Growing up in South Baltimore, I had to fight for my education, battling the stereotype whites held that as a black person I was somehow deficient. I could feel the cinders in my chest begin to glow with a hatred for this colonel, flames that had diminished but not been extinguished from the illegal and retributive punishments meted out recently to black soldiers whose crimes were sometimes fabricated. His insinuation that racism was mine, not his, made me respond angrily.

"What do you think, Captain Coleman?" he spit at me, going formal from the "Jim" he usually called me to send a message that this was an official inquiry.

"Colonel," I responded from miles away, "the Uniform Code of Military Justice is clear, mirroring the United States Constitution we swore to protect. The men have rights, and unless and until they violate the law, they are just as entitled to the presumption of innocence as the whites in this room."

The others looked stunned, as my tone reeked of insubordination. "Cut the shit, Coleman," snarled the colonel, indicating that any semblance of a personal relationship had disappeared. "Find out who their leaders are and let the sergeant major know, and he'll take care of things," the colonel intoned, nodding at his sergeant major, who dutifully made a note on his pad of paper.

Turning away, indicating the meeting was over, he looked briefly at me and added, "That's an order, Captain."

My quest for a successful career in the military to prove blacks could cut it took a hit that day. The idea of a career in law to protect my brothers from the bigoted colonels of the world engulfed my heart as nothing had before.

One of the metrics used to evaluate senior officers—in addition to the infamous body count—was called "time to conviction." The right to due process was a casualty of the Vietnam War. My complicity, though under direct orders, keeps me up nights to this day. The rationale for speedy trials had nothing to do with the rights of the accused. Maintaining manpower levels posed a major challenge, as problems such as foot disease often caused manpower deficits in the pervasive wet mud of the region's rice paddies. Soldiers accused of crimes were held in the Long Binh Jail, which rapidly became overcrowded due to the slow processes of evidence analysis and thorough investigation. Those convicted were needed back in the field once they finished their confinement. I believe that one reason underlying the expedited trials was fear that troublemakers needed to be locked up, especially those embracing the Black Power movement.

My fully adopting civil rights as an issue had a long road to travel. Even Jim Coleman could not support the Black Power movement that had begun spreading in our unit. We identified the leader, and when he stepped out of line, retribution was both swift and sure. Eventually, he was charged with disobeying a direct order during wartime, to wit, as I typed on the charge sheet, he had failed to remove his Black Muslim pendant when ordered to do so. As I wrote Betsy that night, on February 14, 1969:

> We sent our Black Power advocate off to jail today. All his black friends came over to see him off. Instead of shaking hands, they bang fists together. It was really quite a disgusting sight. My friend Jim Coleman was really embarrassed. I kid him about it now, as every time we meet we bang our fists together; how cute.

I attribute the effectiveness of our unit—given the racial tensions—to the incredible dedication of the many career-minded black noncommissioned officers who not only had to deal with inexperienced young officers like me, but also with the unrest among the lower-ranking enlisted men. That we asked black enlistees to risk their lives for a country that, on their return, would limit their access to the polls, offer limited educational opportunities, and consign them to separate facilities makes understandable the anger of so many.

In 1984, when I was a legislator in New Hampshire, the late Nacky Loeb, editor of the notoriously conservative *Manchester Union Leader* (NH), devoted a column to me, calling me a demagogue and a communist sympathizer. She was against my sponsoring a bill that would create the Dr. Martin Luther King Jr. holiday. The bill failed that year by a large margin, though a decade later became law. As the bill's spokesperson, often on the radio, I received threats on my life and the lives of our children largely because they thought I was black.

King could not have known just how "prodigious" those hilltops in New Hampshire, as he described them in his "I have a Dream" speech, would be. New Hampshire did not adopt King's birthday as a holiday until 2000, the last state in the nation to do so.

". . . Let Freedom ring from the prodigious hilltops of New Hampshire . . ."

Martin Luther King Jr. from the "I Have a Dream" speech at the March on Washington, August 28, 1963.

The Dream Lives On
Celebrate Martin Luther King Day in N.H.

Poster presented to Rep. Wayne Burton by NH Chapter of the NAACP for King holiday advocacy

I can never truly know what walking in the shoes of a person of color is like in our country. But for the terrifying moments when I opened anonymous envelopes containing threatening words and demands that I leave the country, all made from letters cut from magazines, I experienced for a few seconds what others endure their entire lives.

Later in life, both to assuage my conscience and to put into play what I had learned about racism, I took an active role in promoting diversity, especially in the last twenty years of my career as Dean of the School of Business at Salem State College and President of North Shore Community College. As a business school dean, I served in several community organizations in the City of Salem, including as chair of the Salem Harbor Community Development Corporation, which promoted affordable housing, education, workforce training, and other programs for more than 2,500 immigrants from the Dominican Republic.

As president of NSCC, which had a large campus in Lynn, Massachusetts, a minority–majority city of 100,000, I joined the Board of the Community Minority Cultural Center (CMCC) at a time when it was beset with serious financial challenges. With the help of resources from the college, the CMCC recovered. During that period, I became good friends with the late Virginia Barton, president of the CMCC board. Ms. Barton, pictured with me at the Dr. Martin Luther King Jr. breakfast, held on the Lynn Campus of North Shore Community College, founded the Lynn chapter of the NAACP. I often turned to Ms. Barton for help in steering the college in directions that would best serve the minority population of Lynn as well as all other students. I feel very fortunate to have known both Captain James Coleman and Virginia Barton.

*The author and Virginia Barton enjoy the program
honoring Dr. Martin Luther King Jr. in 2006 on the Lynn campus
of North Shore Community College*

CHAPTER 4: SHOE POLISH

"Make sure someone checks on Maid who cleans up for CO, XO, ADSO [Assistant Division Signal Officer] prior to lunch each day. Then you will know when she needs shoe polish, soap, etc."
—*Note to author from Executive Officer, January 1, 1969*

"My duties range from reading the latest intelligence summaries on VC activity to making sure the Vietnamese girls don't steal the Major's shoe polish or leave his u-trow [underpants] unwashed."
—*Letter to my wife, January 1, 1969*

"Women in the Special Task Force [Viet Cong]...worked in the American bases. They watched and listened. They were our eyes and ears. That's how we knew what the American officers thought. The women played coy and dumb. All the while, they kept an eye on the officer's maps, and they counted the newly arrived munitions."
—*Viet Cong organizer speaking to Lady Borton "After Sorrow"*

My job as Adjutant of the 9th Signal Battalion, 9th Infantry Division mostly resembled that of an administrative vice president in a civilian corporation though performed under constant threat of rocket and mortar attacks that we experienced almost daily. The job encompassed all the human resource functions including the assignment of incoming troops to our companies, their promotions, evaluations, awards, and keeping of their records. I had no training in the law except in an undergraduate political science course at Bowdoin College, but I served as chief legal officer. In that capacity, I oversaw criminal investigations, drew up charge sheets, and organized special court-martials. The latter were battalion-level tribunals argued before a board of officers who could reduce the accused in rank, fine him, jail him, or all three, depending on the crime. I also handled all requests for compassionate leaves. As our mission included defense of a sector of the base perimeter, I also ran the duty roster for officers commanding the bunkers on the berm at night, pulling that duty myself at least once a week.

Among my least favorite assignments was responsibility for the officers' showers, the BOQs (or hooches) where we lived, and supervising the "hooch girls," local women who cleaned our rooms until we discovered they were gathering intelligence for the Viet Cong. Also, our illegal Officers' Club was unofficially assigned to me. In that capacity, I supervised the club manager, a remarkably resourceful buck sergeant and former bar manager in civilian life, with a drooping black mustache and a similar attitude. Jake procured the best beer and other alcoholic beverages along with movies and great food. The club lacked legal standing in that only one such club was officially authorized for all of Dong Tam. That rule was routinely winked at, both by the army and the navy, who had their own club near the docks on the Mekong River nearby. Our living room–sized space afforded respite from hectic days to talk, eat, drink beer, and watch TV and movies.

The navy club proved very valuable as a source of food, booze, and other items, as their stuff came from the ships offshore. However, they were poor at building bunkers, and one night when they took a direct hit, their walls of corrugated steel turned to flying shrapnel that wounded and killed several men inside. We helped rebuild the club with sandbag blast walls to save lives and protect the steady supply of inventory for our bar.

This sort of bartering occurred not only in the booze business but for war materiel also. The formal procurement systems I had learned from my experience in Germany had given way to straight bargaining in Vietnam. Stationed in Cam Ron Bay, a high-ranking sergeant who I never met but who reported to me, bartered and traded radios, batteries, and miscellaneous items for bullets, beds, and other vital stuff, often with no paperwork backup at all.

My responsibilities included running the "Waiting Wives Club," which consisted of ensuring that my CO sent a letter to the wives of the forty-five or so officers in the battalion every once and a while to assure them of our safety. "I realize how hard a separation of this type is on you and Wayne, as my wife and I are experiencing the same thing," he assured

Betsy in a letter to her. He then lamented, "I can only say the sacrifice you are making is necessary and will never be forgotten. In the final analysis, what you, Wayne, and all Americans in the military service are doing will ensure a better America and a better life for our children and all Americans" (December 29, 1968). He closed the letter urging her to become an active member of the Waiting Wives Club, though I never knew what that meant. And the promise of a better America never materialized.

In addition to ensuring our bunkers were manned 24/7, my two primary functions proved essential—handling awards and decorations and overseeing military justice, the carrot and stick of military culture. Low morale persisted in our unit as one would expect in any military unit at war. Our unclear purpose contributed to the loss of spirit. The antidotes prescribed by our leaders were to award more medals to encourage positive behavior and tighten our military justice processes to discourage bad behavior. In a war in which success was difficult to measure, the career officers competed on awards received. My ability to write recommendations made me indispensable, especially when embellishment, hyperbole, and falsehoods brought success.

Our leaders used the criminal justice system to, among other things, control any hints of insurrection and to try to prevent the rampant drug use afflicting units all over the country, including ours. Since the Uniform Code of Military Justice at that time did not require that soldiers charged with crimes be guaranteed attorneys (the new version in 1972 added that requirement), justice was not always just. For example, I was ordered to ignore the prohibition against officers in the same unit as the accused serving on special courts-martial for men from our battalion. The rules of evidence were often ignored in that the accused were tried before confirmation that a substance was illegal. Black soldiers suspected of fomenting insurrection were especially targeted. That I had to participate in this unjust system is one of my great shames.

From working with the battalion adjutant in my unit in Germany, I also knew that the position included a function not found in the job description: serving as a sounding board for ideas and concerns that could not be presented directly to the commanding officer or executive officer. My desk outside the commander's office at Dong Tam made me the filter for such concerns, a vital function in any organization. My primary NCO served the same function for enlisted men.

This aspect of my job took on great importance under the structure of a signal battalion embedded in an infantry division. The signal battalion CO also served as the full 9th Division Signal Officer, reporting directly to the commanding general. Quite naturally, our CO spent much of his time in his division-level office, leaving day-to-day battalion operations to the battalion executive officer and his direct staff, including me.

In addition to serving as the battalion adjutant, I also served as the headquarters company commander, under which fell the troops in the headquarters, our motor pool, our cooks, and other supporting soldiers including the battalion's combat photographers (who I rarely saw unless they were killed or wounded).

My assignment as pay officer had me flying around the Mekong Delta delivering pay to signal units supporting the troops in the field. I did not mind flying, but in Vietnam, landing had its challenges, an aspect of the war I learned well the first time I flew into Dong Tam. As we approached the base built of mud on the riverbank, I could see the short landing strip out the window across from me in the C-130. Suddenly, the plane tipped to a 90-degree angle to the ground. My side of the plane rolled up so that we hung in the straps on the up side looking down through the windows below. The fast-approaching ground came straight at me as the plane went into a tight downward spiral. I thought it would end in a killing crash. My stomach lodged in my throat and my life flashed in front of my eyes. I hoped my accomplishments during my presence on earth to date would mean something to somebody.

Then, just as suddenly, the plane pulled out of the spiral, hit the runway on its wheels, and bounced to a stop. Noting my green complexion, the NCO who helped me out the door and down the exit ladder explained that ground fire from the ever-present VC surrounding the base could take a plane down if it approached the normal way. A gradual flight path to the airfield, skimming over the landing strip's outskirts, would have taken us right over the area where the VC lay in wait, AKs at the ready to shoot us down. Like the wire-wrapped bus, this experience fueled my anxiety about the war. That kids could blow up buses and the Viet Cong could ambush planes gave lie to the successes being touted in Washington.

It was during one of those early pay runs that I experienced my first encounter with a Vietnamese child, a humanizing moment when I needed it most. As I describe it in my letter to Betsy of December 31, 1968:

As we were driving home on one of these roads around here on which you see mostly American troops, Vietnamese on Hondas, and a few American cars, we were stopped at a bridge. While we were sitting there, about 15 Vietnamese kids came up to the jeep jabbering away. One little boy came up to me and put his hand in mine and rested his head on my knee. He had an English book with him and was trying to talk to me. I wrote my name down in his book and he tried to do his name on his pad. This kid was about 7 years old. I finally gave him my pen, and with that, he was the happiest kid in the world. I showed him how to push the button on the pen to make it write. He thought that was wonderful. It made me feel good, too.

I hope and pray that the year goes by swiftly for us. I know it won't be a good year, at least for the first nine months, but when I remember the look on that kid's face, I can't help but think maybe we are right in helping them.

Binh Luc, the hamlet in which this encounter happened, may well have been cleared by our troops in the months that followed. I truly hope the boy with my pen survived. But I still worry that he did not.

Children on the road seeking "chop-chop" (candy)

My first casualty, though not an actual death, did not result from an incoming rocket or mortar. A smudged report it was that did in my primary NCO, Sergeant First Class Johnson. As I reported to Betsy in my letter of January 9, 1969:

> Bad experience this morning. You know there is a lot of pressure around the HQ here to get things done now! Well today it really piled up. There's this thing we're trying to get ready to send forward called an M.U.C.—Meritorious Unit Citation. Well, it's taken us three weeks off and on to get it ready. It's about 30 pages, and each one had to be retyped about 20 times because it must be perfect. Well, after four nights' work, we finally thought we had it right. So I brought it in to the major for approval, and he found one smudge on a page and said to retype it. I brought it back to SFC Johnson, my administration MCO, and he couldn't believe it. He said he wanted to quit because he couldn't take it anymore. I told him to relax and take it easy. Next thing I know, the guy completely broke down crying and everything. It was pitiful. He had a nervous breakdown right in my office. I tried to help him, but finally we got a doctor and they took him away. I feel very badly because he was trying so hard and the major found one smudge. God Damn Army! Anyway, now I'll have to struggle on alone.

My CO was pleased that we ultimately received that citation. He ordered me to ensure a copy made it into his personnel file. SFC Johnson did return to work but was never the same. It was just the incredible pressure of preparing the documents on manual typewriters, but as he later confided in me, being a man of integrity, he felt guilty knowing that much of what the report contained was bullshit. For example, the closing paragraph I penned in the Recommendation for Award of Meritorious Unit Commendation reads:

> The operational success of the 9th Signal Battalion paralleled the building of esprit de corps among its officers and men. Indicative of this esprit is the low rate of AWOLs, Article 15s and courts-martial. The number of personal decorations earned by the members of the 9th Signal Battalion during the period cited by

this recommendation also reflects the high spirit maintained by the units of the 9th Signal Battalion.

I served with good soldiers trying to do their best under dreadful conditions for a vague cause. But I do not believe I had any data to support the assertions in that paragraph. What we did have was a commander vying for promotion to full colonel, and in the US Army, a superb presentation seemed more important than fact when many lower-ranking field-grade officers vied for fewer and fewer slots in the upper ranks.

The day Sergeant Johnson returned, he seemed to be holding it together. I described it to Betsy this way:

Last night as I was walking to dinner, he walked by going the other way. We of course let him off for yesterday afternoon, and I hadn't seen him all that time. Well anyway, his eyes were red and he was still crying. I turned around and went after him. I caught up with him and sort of led him over to my hooch. He kept crying and saying what a frustrating job it is and that he can't live up to the standards that have been set. Well, I tried to comfort him, and I got a couple of beers and we had a long talk. I got my friend Jim Coleman…to come in and talk to him because they had been good friends. Anyway, we sat and talked to this guy for three hours. Finally we convinced him that he should stay and stick it out because if he quit now, he'd never be the same. Well, happy ending—he came back to work this morning and although he was tense, naturally, because everyone had seen him break down, he worked steadily and seemed to have regained his composure.

It really shook me up, though, first to see a 37-year-old sergeant bawling his eyes out, and secondly because it showed me what the pressure here can do to a guy. It doesn't bother me, though, because I'm getting out. We have five West Pointers here who are staying in, and they must do well. I have a distinct advantage over them.

CHAPTER 5: SHOOTING IN THE DARK

I'm using a starlight scope tonight. This is a telescopic device which magnifies the lights off the stars and enables one to see in the dark. I can see everything even though it's pitch dark. I've also shot up a few places as some of the guards think they see people. It turned out to be their imagination.

—Letter to my wife, January 21, 1969

We hated getting hit during our bar time between 9:30 or so and 11:00 at night, which is probably why the VC attacked then, not to mention having the cover of darkness. But ROTC did not teach what I would be up against at midnight on January 11, 1969, as I related to Betsy.

We were hit last night by mortars while most of the officers were in the bar. I stumbled from my stool when the siren went off and went running back to my hooch and put on my flack vest and helmet. I grabbed my rifle and took off for my company, where I'm supposed to be during attacks. The first thing I did was trip over about five officers who were lying on the ground. They cursed me furiously, but I stumbled on.

When I got to the bunker where my troops were supposed to be, I found the guys lying around in their underwear smoking and bitching because they had to get out of the billets. Well, it was 12:00 at night so no one could see my rank. I announced who I was and tried to get them all into the bunker. It seems that a lot of the new people don't realize the danger. Isn't that amazing! They almost think it's another form of harassment.

Anyway, I finally got them into the bunker when I noticed this white form moving around the top of a water tower. It turned out to be one of my clerks, named Lindstrom, who is my aesthetic. He said he always climbs the water tower during attacks so he can watch the shells come in and go out. I admit it is sort of pretty, but I tried to explain to him that it was safer on the ground. Not only that, but he was nude and was swimming around in the tower, which holds drinking water. This guy is funny. I asked what he was doing up there, and he said, "Why, I was swimming, Sir," as if I was stupid. I said "Why?" and he said, "Because I feel safer up there." What could I say? It probably is sort of refreshing to float on your back and watch the shells go over.

Lindstrom turned out to be one of my best clerks. He declared himself a "Jack Mormon," meaning fallen away from the Mormon Church. If a different viewpoint was needed in any discussion, I would ask Lindstrom for his. I was never disappointed.

My enlisted guys caused fewer problems for me than the officers, as I reported to Betsy on January 12, 1969:

Things took a turn for the worse today as a new major arrived to take over S-3. He keeps bitching about his room—his locker is not big enough and all this crap. We have five new officers coming in, and I don't have enough room in my BOQ for them, so I'm going to have to put the lowest-ranking men together so the major can live alone. Boy, will that piss a few people off. Last night, the generators went off leaving no power and no water. Consequently, there was no water in the officers' shower, for which I was castigated and had to go out at 2 a.m. with a tanker to procure water. My job as adjutant is good, as we've finally caught up with everything, but my company needs some work and I just don't have the time. Also, today is Sunday, which I guess used to be a day of rest back in the world. I went over to get my pictures today and guess what—the PX is closed for inventory.

I often think that whatever success I later achieved as an academic dean and then a college president supporting faculty members went back to my days supporting military officers who were just as cranky. As I observe to Betsy in the same letter:

We had a big rebellion in the lounge last night because the lieutenants don't like the way the field-grade officers run our little club, i.e., no shower shoes or T-shirts. I could care less, but it's fun watching people nit-pick about nothing. Watching people work under stress is more fun than watching people under normal conditions.

Things were looking up as I also reported: "I'm finally getting rid of my housekeeping detail. The colonel's making this captain named Graham the HHD commander…He's from Tennessee and is very nervous and insecure. He spent his first six months here in the infantry, which accounts for his nervousness, and he's a southern OCS officer who is…staying in."

Many of my letters contained very personal stuff that should not be public. But sex was a topic in many of my letters, just as it was in the orderly room, the officers' club, and elsewhere. It even snuck into my report on my reading habits when I related them to Betsy in my letter of January 13, 1969.

I've just started reading Steinbeck's *Winter of Our Discontent*, and I'm enjoying it. I think I told you that we had quite an extensive library in my orderly room, so I should be able to read a lot of the stuff I never read before. Believe me, I'm not getting psycho, but I do find it somewhat enjoyable. I must admit I do think of sex occasionally, but I can't think of it in any other terms but you, which makes me very happy. It makes me happy because it puts me apart from the guys who think only of sex in general. I just miss you, dear, mentally and physically. I get depressed sometimes, but I have your picture and your letters.

In that same letter, I acknowledged adopting another dog, a mongrel named George, to help keep me sane. In the next night's letter, I noted that one of our many dogs had had a litter, and my troops were taking care of them.

We have a big dog problem over here. I mean a big large-dog problem—you know what I mean. There's a pack of dogs here, and yesterday one of them bit one of the gooks in the ass. For some reason, these dogs hate Vietnamese girls. It's sort of sad, though, to try and get rid of the dogs because a lot of them are puppies. But the colonel said they must go, so they must go. I can see his point, but the troops get attached to the dogs and it's sort of tough. Bruno did not like hiding in my hooch after that. But I knew my CO was "short," with a month or so left in his tour. So Bruno and I sought to outlast him.

George and Bruno nap next to the author's desk in the battalion HQ

In that letter, I reported in the same tone that during the previous night's mortar attack, the VC had blown up our PX. The normalization of the combat around us, much like talking about the weather, constituted another mechanism to ward off the abject fear and bladder-emptying terror we really felt as the explosions walked toward whatever shelter we took when the sirens went off. The best example of assimilating mayhem into our everyday activities comes in a letter to Betsy on March 10, 1969.

We have a general coming for a cocktail party at our new club tonight. I had to plan the thing around the enemy mortar attacks, though, as we're scheduled to get hit about 7 o'clock. The mortar attacks usually last about 45 minutes, so I scheduled the thing for 8. Doesn't this sound crazy? But it's true.

How many event planners must schedule around an assault? And yes, I had begun thinking about preserving my own sanity. Perhaps to break up the monotony of the ton of paperwork and other tasks, I would visit the villages around the base during the day when it was relatively safe. I reported on those to Betsy in my letters like this one from January 19, 1969:

Must tell you of my sojourn through the villages today. They have the biggest, fattest hogs I have ever seen. I saw a pregnant sow who would almost come to mid-thigh on me; amazing. Second observation was the way these little tiny kids ride these huge water buffaloes. The horns on the buffaloes go straight back from their heads like this (drawing of head) and the kids sit under the horns with reins hooked into [the animal's] nose. Another thing is the number of ducks they have. Swarms of ducks all over the rice paddies. I don't know if they are imported, but they sure look like American ducks."

Boy leading his water buffalo to the field for work

After another trip around our neighboring hamlets I observed, "The Vietnamese don't have any running water, of course—they have a well or a river. One day I saw a woman washing clothes, a woman cleaning food, and a boy whizzing all in the same stream. These people just don't know what sanitation is because nobody's shown them."

A village on a Mekong tributary serving many purposes

Surrealism surfaces again in the range of activities and feelings I convey to Betsy in my letter of January 21, 1969: "I'm writing tonight from the Command Post of our perimeter defense. It's like OD [Officer of the Day] except I'm in charge of 11 bunkers that stretch along one sector of the perimeter. It looks like this. I'm presently at the sixth bunker from the right looking out over a cleared area into a jungle.

The VC haven't attacked this place by land in quite a while so there's no sweat, but I've got two machine guns above me for protection."

I continue with a non sequitur: "I received my card back from the National Testing Service, so I take the GMAT [Graduate Management Admissions Test] on the 1st of February [Betsy's birthday month]. I'll probably go up to Saigon Friday and stay overnight, as the test is at 7:30 in the morning. I'll be studying Friday night. I haven't had a chance to study too much, so I don't have great hopes. If I don't get over 500, I'm not applying. If I do, I will apply."

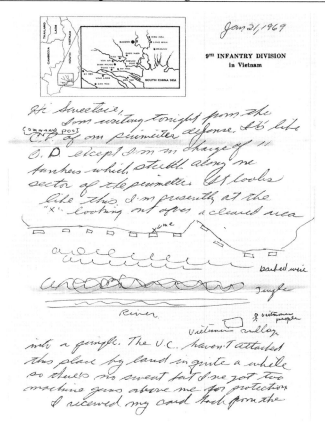

Diagram of defensive bunkers in Dong Tam base camp berm

Then, responding to an earlier inquiry from her, I write, "You asked about TV. Yes, we do get American shows—some of which are good. We don't get Don Rickles, although I do remember him. The single best gesture you could make would be to send a TV over, as the only one we have is in the lounge and no one can really watch it. If you think it would be too much trouble to send, don't bother, but I sure would like to have that little one."

I proceed from TVs to insects. "There are a lot of mosquitoes in this damn bunker. More than I've seen over here. Our hooches are well sprayed. I have a can of repellant beside my bed and am deadly with it. I'm down to one *swoosh* per mosquito. They have some great insects here. It seems like all the New England insects, only twice as big. I had a cricket-looking thing in my hooch today that was nearly three inches long. I figure if I can housebreak it, I'll keep it for a pet. Would you believe Chris Cricket?"

Wrapping up the disjointed missive romantically, I wrote, "Well, I must make my rounds and make sure our people are awake. It's pretty tonight, as it usually is, because the sky is always clear and there are thousands of stars. It's nice, too, because I know that you look at the same sky, so we're not completely apart." But I close with the war: "Truth is I do not know if the shadows moving in my starlight scope were my imagination, trees, or people. I hope they were one of the first two or both. But in any event, I kept firing the 50-caliber machine gun until the image disappeared from the screen in my scope."

On January 22, 1969, I report to Betsy that "The last mortar attack, three men were killed and 23 were wounded. The VC are long shots, though, and seem to just aim at Dong Tam, which is three-quarters of a mile square. Last night, they destroyed our brand-new movie theater. Fortunately, no one was in it, there were men needed in other places."

Branching out to the "big picture": "The powers-that-be thought that Charlie (VC) was going to stage an attack on Saigon coincident with Nixon's inauguration. It did not come off, however, and now they're wondering whether or not a Tet Offensive will take place."

The next paragraph leads with a warning label: "My next paragraph deals with how much I miss you. Sometimes I roll over in bed thinking I'll find you there, and all I do is hit the wall. How awful. I never thought I could miss anyone so much, but I do. There's no getting around it. Thinking I'll be back this year and all the other rationalizations won't fill the emptiness I feel not having you with me."

CHAPTER 6: ORPHANS

We sponsor an orphanage in My Tho, about five miles from here, for little Vietnamese kids. I plan to go down there Sunday and play with the kids and bring them some candy. No matter how this war comes out, these are the kids that lose. I guess if we can show them some kindness, they may grow up to like Americans. Heaven knows America can use it.

—Letter to my wife, January 30, 1969

Ho awaits the author's arrival standing tall

In January, I caught a tremendous break when our unbearably arrogant executive officer finished his tour and was replaced by Jim Caddigan, an outgoing guy with a good sense of humor from my home area of Boston. We became good friends as well as colleagues. He had spent the first six months of his tour in Vietnam in a staff job in Saigon, never seeing combat. Helping him adapt to life under fire fell to me as his primary report. As I explained to Betsy in my letter of January 21, 1969:

> I received your letter of Jan. 14th today, and would like you to know that my sense of humor has never been better—we keep each other laughing here because it's all we have to make life bearable. When situations get tense, somebody usually breaks the ice with a snappy remark—and it's usually me. Major Caddigan, our new XO, is great. He has a sense of humor, is a real good officer, and he's disillusioned with the army. Last night, he asked me why I didn't go RA [Regular Army]. I said I didn't want to, and he said OK. No pep talks, no questions—I respect him for that.

Jim directed television shows before joining the military, an interest no doubt related to his father's work directing Lowell Thomas adventure shows. Jim directed a portion of the old Jackie Gleason shows, as well as NFL football games. He could get angry when something went awry—like the time my clerk failed to show up in time for a court-martial or when I blew a proofread of one of his letters. "Major Caddigan makes me laugh when he gets mad, though, which makes him madder," I wrote to Betsy. Jim Coleman, Jim Caddigan, and I became a threesome, often finding each other when solving issues in the unit or just to have fun. The ungodly hours, the threat of assaults, and the disillusionment with our purpose could easily drag even officers into depressive pits. Having buddies to prop you up at those moments was critical to both performance and emotional well-being.

My relationship with Jim Coleman will always be special for me. As it turned out, Jim's law school exam was rescheduled, so I traveled to Saigon to take the Graduate Management Admissions Test by myself with a group from my motor pool along for protection. We left early in the morning for the twenty-mile trip, but only *after* our engineers had cleared Highway 4 of the mines the VC laid every night. We traveled through two villages that had experienced recent combat, including one with a pile of Vietnamese bodies. Sniper rounds pinged by me at one point, and my men returned fire at the tree where a muzzle flash had been spotted. I hope I had regrets over endangering my men's lives for my exam, but suspect I did not. Being in danger was a way of life.

As we entered Saigon, we headed for Tudo Street, a favorite of Americans packed with bars and other establishments favored by our troops. I described it to Betsy in my letter as "an anthill where all the ants have motorbikes—just millions of…people going all over the place. I am in Vitoria Hotel with tube and study book for the evening."

My motor pool took a room down the hall from me, and soon the noise of partying came through the walls, rock-and-roll music and squealing women. I made sure all my men had taken the "no sweat" pills issued by our corpsman that were supposed to prevent venereal disease.

As I rehearsed answering possible test questions, a tentative knock came at my door. I snapped on my .45 pistol and cracked open the door to see a slight woman of very young age begging to enter my room. I began to close the door when she pleaded with me to allow her in because if I did not, her mama-san selling sexual services in the hotel would beat her. Feeling sympathetic, I allowed her to come in if she would agree to sit in the chair by the door for fifteen or twenty minutes and then leave. Gratefully, she agreed, slipping into the room and taking her place by the door. I continued studying for the exam, only looking up when I heard the door close behind her when she left.

I'm not sure why this incident became important to me. Certainly, as a product of the '50s, watching my mother give up her career as a concert pianist to do our family laundry reinforced the sexism I'd acquired in my youth and continued into my early twenties. But something about the spirit of the Vietnamese women and my sympathy with those in bondage to the sex trade began my attitudinal journey from borderline misogyny to embracing gender equality. Unknowingly, the list of assumptions I had carried into Vietnam were shattered with experiences such as this.

My report to Betsy upon returning to my base on the Mekong reads as follows:

> Saigon was very depressing—it really has a stench all its own. It reminds me of a filthy Rome. There is nothing beautiful in it. I went into a sidewalk shop for a cup of coffee with this navy lieutenant who was also taking the test. I ordered coffee and received this black liquid that tasted like hot liquid pepper. After I gagged

for ten minutes, this little man brought me a cup of tea, which wasn't too bad. It was fascinating to watch the people eating with their chopsticks. They caught me staring a few times, but it was worth it. You'd have a nervous breakdown if you had to even ride in the city. There are thousands of motorbikes all over the streets. The cabs are little Fiats. (drawing of little car) They also have motorbike cabs that look like (drawing) or so. Then you have your assorted army tanks, jeeps, [deuce-and-a-halfs], etc., and there are no traffic lights to speak of or cops.

February 2, 1969, raised my spirits as the mail brought relief.

I received your care package today and have already eaten all the nibbles. Major Caddigan, Jim Coleman, and I gathered at the club and ate the tortilla crackers (voted favorite over cocktail sticks) for our supper. Your chocolate chip cookies came at just the right time, as I think I was about to turn cold fish over lack of sweets. My mother's spice squares arrived simultaneously, so I do believe I've gained about 20 lbs. today.

In the same letter I gave her an update on my future. "I sent the letters asking for recommendations today, as my application cannot be considered until all the paperwork is in. That includes test results, recommendations, and application. I've got it planned so they all land together. The deadline for applications is July 1st, so there is no sweat there." In a previous missive, I had noted that I had all the information I needed to leave military service with a resignation letter the next June. Surviving the next ten months became the challenge. The next day's letter included an ominous prediction.

A lot of action around here lately. They think one last big communist push is coming, so old Dong Tam is up in arms. I don't get too shaken up about things until I see them though. You can imagine what the rumor mill is like here.

My admonition proved prophetic, as over the next few weeks, my letters describe daily rocket and mortar attacks. One letter describes the action I missed:

Last night was a bad one for old Dong Tam, as Charlie really put the schnitzel to us. I guess this is what everyone was expecting, but it was still a shock. Here at Dong Tam, about 20 men were killed and 90 wounded. They attacked us at 2:30 in the morning and kept it up, off and on, until 1:00 in the afternoon. They even tried to rush the place but were driven back. I went out in my mail truck (as I have no jeep as such, I use this mail truck, which is a converted ambulance—quite funny, actually) and surveyed the damage.

The author surveys the damage from converted mail truck

Some buildings were demolished, with thousands of holes where the shrapnel went through. They also hit this huge diesel fuel storage tank, which exploded and burned in spectacular fashion for about 18 hours. And do you want to hear the kicker—I SLEPT THOUGH THE WHOLE THING! Yes, dear, the first

I knew what was going on was when I dragged my ass out of the sack at 7:30 this morning. The first thing I saw was this roaring diesel fire, which I thought was really [the result] of someone putting too much oil on the human waste. We burn all human waste on Dong Tam, which adds to the wonderful bouquet of the already pungent Delta. Anyway, here's this fire and everyone running around with weapons and war togs, so I finally stopped this guy and asked him what the hell was going on. He then told me that we had been under attack for four hours and could not believe that I had been in bed all that time—some of the bullets hit the side of the BOQ and five mortar rounds hit right up the street in the hospital. Anyway, everyone thinks I am nerveless because I sleep through attacks. Actually, between you and me, I have these two old warrant officer friends, Mr. Tucker, the brother of the Mr. Tucker from Germany who lives next door to me, and a Mr. Addams. They're both good friends of mine, and last night I went over to Chief Tucker's at his request to have a few lagers and listen to CW (country & western). I don't like CW all that well, but since he is my next-door neighbor, and old Wayne has never been known to turn down a free beer, I went over and had quite a few with them; hence my deep "sleep." In the future, Sergeant Johnson is going to come over and make sure I'm up. From what I've heard, about 100 camps were hit around the country, so I suppose this will keep up for a while. Do not fret for my safety, as I am no hero and will get into the bunker next time, when I wake up.

The tragedy of the whole thing is that the swimming pool was closed down and I couldn't get in my noonly swim.

My emotional offset from the grind of work under the cloud of attacks came from a source I had not expected—kids. One of my many responsibilities was as our unit's Civic Actions Officer. No easy responsibility to fulfill when our primary focus remained killing as many communists as we could. As previously stated, I had written to Betsy about it, and in April I wrote to our neighbors in Belmont who had helped my mother run a clothing drive at their church to support the orphanage.

Dear Nat and Kaye,

I really appreciate your help on the clothes for the orphanage. It's sad and heartwarming at the same time to see these kids who have known nothing but war since birth. The young Americans don't know how well off they are. You really must see a place like Vietnam to appreciate the luxury of living in the US.

The American way of life is completely incomprehensible to the Vietnamese, which is one reason I'm not sure they could ever live under a government system such as ours. They are happy people but need guidance and direction; if nothing else, I hope this war provides that.

The kids at the orphanage are no different from American children. They sing, play games, get fresh, and ask for candy and all the other things associated with kids. Every Sunday, a truckload of food and men go to the orphanage and distribute these items they need to the children. The orphanage is run by Vietnamese nuns, and also houses adults who are mentally retarded. I admire the sisters so much. I can't imagine what hard work they must do to take care of all their charges.

Two nuns in the My Tho orphanage display clothes
sent by the author's parents from a clothing drive at their church
in Belmont, Massachusetts

My letter to Betsy described one of our visits:

Today we went to the orphanage. I packed up my camera, rifle, pistol, helmet, flak jacket, and off we went. I also brought the candy you sent me—I don't eat too many hard candies and knew the kids would love them. Anyway, we got to My Tho safely after stopping in the center of the town to take some pictures. It's a typical grubby, incongruently [built] town with millions of people and sidewalk shops and markets. It is right on the Mekong River, however, and I did get a lot of good shots of the city....

We went to the orphanage, which at one time was a poor man's manor. It had a gate, which was opened on our arrival. Everywhere one looked, there were bullet holes in the walls, etc., from last year's Têt. Anyway, there are 400 orphans there ranging in age from four months to 15 years old. There are also older people who are mentally retarded. The girls all come up and grab a GI and stick with him. They reminded me of pigeons in St. Mark's on Farragut Square. This one little urchin named Ho—6 ½ years old—latched on to my little finger and dragged me around, showing me all the scenic wonders. She was real cute but a strong-willed little girl. I piggybacked her around and got all tired out, as she called in her friends and I played with them also.

About this time, the truck came from the battalion with the week's rations for the orphanage, and soon there were about 15 or 20 GIs playing with the kids and laughing and giggling. I don't know who benefited the most. I gave out all the candy, and everybody loved it. So your candy found its way into some little orphan's mouth, dear. During this time, they played games and a GI played the guitar. It was quite refreshing. Ho showed me her room and made me sit down at her little tea table—she was about 2½ feet tall. She then brought out her scrapbook and showed me all the pages. This sounds light and cheery, and it was.

Then she walked me into a different section, and I saw the most horrible forms of humanity I've ever seen. There was a kid with teeth sticking out every which way from his mouth. His head was deformed, and he sat on the ground and pulled himself along sliding on his ass. He had these heavy leather pants on for this purpose. He was about 20, I guess, and when I walked by, he giggle-gurgled at me. I almost puked. Then I saw some little kids throwing stones at some of the deranged adults.

Well, for the most part it was nice. They gave us Cokes and stuff, and I took 12 prints and 20 slides of the trip.

The author is greeted on arrival by a nun and a group of residents at the My Tho orphanage

Bullet holes from the 1968 TET offensive pockmark the door of the My Tho Orphanage

The author playing with the children at the orphanage

One of the author's men enjoys the adoration of a small girl as they meander around the orphanage grounds

On the way home, we stopped at a small PX outside My Tho, about 15 miles from Dong Tam. We parked the jeep outside and left our weapons, camera, and other equipment with one man as guard. This PX is on the main road and is set up for a group of American advisors to the Vietnamese Army, which has an HQ in My Tho. Anyway, I went into this small fortress, bought more film and a traveling bag for $1.80, and left. When I came out, a bunch of little kids were around the jeep as they usually are. Suddenly, one little boy grabs my camera, the Minolta Instamatic, and takes off. Well, we couldn't catch him, and all the Viets were staring at us, so I had to let him go. It happens quite frequently, though, that these kids are bad. They found out a little boy of 10 who had been a mascot for an infantry outfit over here was working for the VC and was responsible for the deaths of 80 Americans. Anyway, it kind of spoiled my day.

I did not report to Betsy that I had unholstered my .45 and aimed it at the back of the thief's head as he took off. Looking back, that moment when I almost shot a boy remained with me more than others. I knew, with body count so important, that rather than being prosecuted for a crime, I would be credited with a kill. My violent side and my peaceful side warred in my head over what was right. The latter won out, as it would continue to do over the remainder of my term in Vietnam. I remember thinking, "It's only a camera." In my letter to Betsy, I try to make sense of the "paradoxes and inconsistencies" of my situation. The army had trained me to perform amorally, following orders with no questions. But the human conscience is not easily silenced. As I tried to explain in my letter:

It wasn't so much the camera as it is the frightening feeling that the Americans are suckers and the Vietnamese think of us that way. I know if the situations were reversed, would the Orientals help us? Hell no. I think the Vietnamese do not understand our altruistic motives and think we are crazy and therefore suckers. Obviously that's not true for all of them, but I think the majority are used to poverty, ignorance, filth, etc. I don't really know if they want more. What we're doing is like taking the 18th-century pioneer and forcing him [to become] a 20th-century suburbanite. Can't be done, dear. True, we can help them and probably should, but make no mistake about it, the Vietnamese do not really appreciate our help or the reasons for it. In their day-to-day existence, we're just a rare gold mine in the dump. I'm not saying we shouldn't be here, I'm just saying our reasons for being here are not in tune with why the Vietnamese want us. I wish I were with you, so I could ramble on. What it boils down to is it is quite an interesting situation full of paradoxes and inconsistencies that also could describe the oriental mind.

The orphanage itself, which would become a major issue later in my tour, held its own paradox. Many of the kids seemed to be of mixed races. Those whose fathers were black were more obvious than those appearing to be of mixed Asian/Caucasian parentage. That the children came into the world this way had to do in part with the army's not prohibiting sexual relations with native Vietnamese, but actually abetting them.

We knew that across the river to our west was a "friendly" village, one classified that way by our intelligence and one on which we were prohibited from firing even though mortar-tube muzzle flashes could be seen that indicated the enemy used the village as a firing base. It was also a place GIs could find sexual gratification though risking disease. As I described it to Betsy:

> The troopies do sleep with them but have to pay for it. Since Dong Tam is a restricted area, the troopies go down to the river on the west side of Dong Tam. They whistle, and a little boat comes across with a girl in it. The boat picks the GI up and brings him across to the Vietnamese side. Anyway, they do it, pay the girl, and normally pick up VD. We tell these guys and tell these guys, but they get so damn horny they don't care.

I believe it is the moral murkiness that later leads to post-traumatic stress disorder, substance abuse, and suicide in veterans coping with what they did after they did it. While in Vietnam, our dogs helped keep me sane.

> I fed George and Bozo—his brother—the dog candy you sent. Bozo is smarter than George (who is a bitch, by the way) and can now sit up after five weeks of life. Under my tutelage, I will bring her into stardom as I did with Trinket—with a little help from you, of course.

About the dogs, we give them to a kennel here in Saigon so they're all right. The trouble is, some of these dogs have rabies because they all can't be vaccinated.

During this period, an incident happened that was typical of Vietnam at that time, and I wrote about it to Betsy.

We were listening on the tactical radios last night (like the one in my jeep in Germany) and heard this guy calling in identifying himself as a prisoner of war. He said he had been captured in September by the VC and had just escaped. They checked his story at Division HQ and found that a guy with his name had been listed as disarmed and missing. His battery finally gave out and they went out looking for him in helicopters. They still haven't found him yet, but he provided some excitement around the battalion.

About a week later, I checked with our intelligence people and was advised the guy was not heard from again.

Toward the end of February, we suffered some of the heaviest assaults of my tour. In my letter of February 24th, I told Betsy, "Things are popping as Dong Tam is surrounded." But I assure her, "Actually the safest place to be is on the berm (what we call the perimeter), as the mortars usually hit on the base, not the edge. If the VC attack, I'll have helicopters on call to come swooping in, so no sweat here." The assaults let up at the end of February, and we temporarily went off yellow alert, which had indicated an attack was imminent.

I suspect our bravado hiding the ever-present fear can best be illustrated by my report to Betsy on the status of the remodeling of our officers' club. "The roof over the patio is almost completed, and this month's Hail and Farewell this Friday night will be its grand opening. I am presently getting some steaks from the mess hall, and we will barbecue them outdoors, so it should be a good time—naturally, because I'm running it."

CHAPTER 7: INCOMING

I got a letter tonight from Dad B., which just about floored me. He has never written me before, mainly because he is too shy or something. Anyway, it was a very good letter with news of home. He mentioned how much he enjoyed seeing you on Easter and other things. I could tell it was an effort for him. I think I make him nervous or something.

—Letter to Betsy about letter from my father,
April 18, 1969

As the battalion's "Chief Personnel Officer," I was not involved in the strategic planning of combat operations other than the personnel implications and planning changes for protecting the berm. As General Hunt notes in his book, the base defense was left to "clerks, cooks, mechanics, and others [who] constantly manned the base camp perimeters and were subjected to direct fire attacks by the enemy on many occasions." Having been initially successful in massive assaults on American and South Vietnamese forces during the first Tet Offensive in 1968, the North Vietnamese Army and their VC allies hoped to replicate their effort in February and March of 1969. The 1968 operation was ultimately beaten back with heavy VC and NVA losses, but it did give the North Vietnamese negotiating team engaged in the Paris Peace Talks additional leverage.

Much of this was lost on us because we judged our situation by the level of combat, the number and intensity of the attacks, on our base. March of 1969 became the most intense month of the war for us as the NVA and VC hammered away at us with rocket and mortar fire, mostly at night and less frequently during the day. Elements of the 9th were deployed constantly into the surrounding area and conducted hundreds of helicopter assaults on suspected hostile hamlets in the Delta. As Ken Burns reports in his video documentary, The Vietnam War, "Patrols would pursue the enemy around the clock. The night sky was full of helicopters, some armed with equipment that could detect the presence of carbon and ammonia, which meant human beings were present but not which side they were on." It didn't matter, as they were shot anyway.

A brief end-of-February respite ended as the attacks resumed a few days later, on March 2nd. The next day, I reported to Betsy:

> Last night we were attacked at 12:00 midnight and had just got-ten the all-clear when the sirens went off again and back we went into the bunkers. This time, we were notified that the red alert (under attack) would last all night. I must admit I provided most of the entertainment with corny jokes. Major Jim would dump on me and I would give it back to him. About three a.m. we all finally lay down on the floor and slept. Most of the incoming landed around Division HQ with nary a one in our area. At one point, I had to poo so bad I left the bunker and went to the john. Major Jim says he's going to give me a purple heart for having diarrhea in the middle of an attack. So everyone is quite beat tonight and hoping we won't have to spend tonight in the bunker. I'm carrying my air mattress around with me just in case.

A lull in the attacks followed, and on March 4th, I noted that for the first time in a week, according to our intelligence, an attack was not immi-nent—though I wore my steel helmet and flak jacket at my desk as I did paperwork. I remember envying soldiers in wars of old with planned bat-tles against conventional enemies in which troops were sent into combat then pulled back to safe rear areas for respite. No safe rear areas existed in Vietnam, so the threat of injury or death was with us always. If I as an officer felt emotional stress born of wariness and exacerbated by wea-riness from lack of peaceful sleep, our enlisted people were stressed out even more.

A shelling hiatus lasted just a few days, and on March 9th I told Betsy, "I guess the VC have a thing about Saturday nights, as we were under major attack from 12 to 3 a.m., which caused great lack of sleep. Also, they hit that damn fuel tank again, and once more the skies above

Dong Tam were filled with fire. Nobody was hurt in the battalion area, although 15 were wounded on the whole of Dong Tam."

Between red alerts, we frequently received visitors who would fly in for briefings and leave as soon as they could for safer areas. Some visits were memorable, like this one:

Last night was the big general's reception, and everything went quite smoothly. This general named Rienzi is the most amazing character I have ever met. He shook everybody's hand in the place (there were 50 officers in attendance) and asked them what they did. He really was a character. He knew a bunch of our West Pointers, and they started reminiscing about some party they had at Ft. Monmouth. It seems they had a party one time and they ended it with steak and beer at midnight. Well one of the LTs asked him if he would like to come back at midnight last night and have some eggs and beer. He said sure, and everybody laughed because of course he was kidding. Anyway, the hard core was in the lounge at 11:30 last night talking things over (Coleman, WO Adams, WO Stamm, Fred Beshore, and myself = hard core. Just for last night; I'm not drinking very much actually) when the general walked in wanting to know where his eggs and beer were. When we recovered, we directed him to the mess hall, and there we did, in fact, eat fried eggs and a couple of beers with this crazy general. He's about 6'7" tall to start with; you would have loved this guy.

On March 14th, I did ask Betsy to reassure my mother that I was OK. Articles had appeared in the Boston papers describing "battered Dong Tam." Some had photos of the massive fires engulfing parts of our camp when our ammo dump and fuel tanks were hit. I did send her pictures from the *Stars and Stripes* Vietnam edition. One was about the Secretary of Defense "who blessed us with his presence. I hope he liked staying in a bunker for two hours, as we were hit the night he was here." Must have made it tough to tell President Nixon we were winning as was reported in American newspapers. The page I sent her also reported that we had "knocked off 1300 VC. What a stupid way to say it's good, by saying the ratio was 16 to 1 [enemy to Americans killed]. It wasn't so damn good for that 1 American." Looking back, it wasn't so damn good for those 16 Vietnamese, either.

Since body count by itself did not impress without context, the kill ratio index was emphasized. To maximize the impact, the numerator of that fraction had to be exaggerated while the denominator was understated, the pernicious effect of a war measured by deaths.

Between January and July, roughly the period I served in the 9th in Vietnam, according to Major General Hunt Jr. (The 9th Infantry Division in Vietnam) we had a kill ratio of nearly 50 to 1. His data show 14,861 enemy dead compared to 300 Americans killed, though we also suffered 4,400 wounded. The 9th, according to his data for the full period it was in Vietnam (February 1967–July 1969), claimed 31,136 enemy dead while incurring 1,869 Americans killed. Wounded numbered 16,232.

My usual attempt to allay concerns at home received a setback in the subject in my letter of March 18th:

> About attacks and stuff, they have agents out in the boonies who pass information to us, so we sometimes know when an attack is coming. Of course, 50% of the time the reports are wrong. Every time we are attacked, we fire right back at them with our own mortars and stuff. Also, the helicopter gunships go out and shoot back at them. It really looks like the 4th of July. The VC are usually shot or captured. When I was on the berm, we fired at some people who were sniping at us. I don't know if I hit anything or not. They were firing at the next bunker from mine, so there was no danger."

Truth was, I had no way of knowing who the VC snipers were shooting at, as the rounds whistled around our bunker, some hitting the sandbags with a resounding *whump!*

I tried to minimize the danger, just as we did in country, by attempting to "normalize" the assaults. On March 19th, my letter described my anger at having the VC interrupt our viewing of our favorite TV show, the ground-breaking *Laugh-In*. "Yes, *Laugh-In* is the highlight of the week here in the 9th Sig. Last week, we had just settled in for a night of merriment when some rounds came in and it was to the bunkers for almost an hour. When we got back, all that was left was the last skit in the wall.

Everyone was quite upset." And I certainly wouldn't allow the VC to ruin my first beer of the night, as I relate on March 21st: "We've already been hit slightly tonight during supper time. I was in the lounge having my post-dinner beer when the siren went off. Glad to report I did not spill a drop of beer as I went the 25-odd yards or so to the bunker."

We did not think about the politics of why we were there as much as one might think, distracted as we were by our long workdays and periods under attack. But while my CO was away, I represented him at the commanding general's briefing in an air-conditioned underground bunker. Walking into the facility was like strolling into a room in the Pentagon. The tiled floors, recessed lighting, painted walls, conditioned air, and untanned briefing officers with nearly transparent skin could easily have been in Washington as in the Mekong Delta. I described the experience to Betsy in my letter of March 21st:

> I attended the general's briefing tonight just for the hell of it and was quite impressed. The floors of the big briefing room are polished just before the general comes in, then everyone stands up when [he] walks in along with his two assistant generals. The briefing covers all the division activities and lasts about an hour. Here is where all the strategy is worked out, and it is quite interesting as they move men around on the map to where they should go to kill the most VC. It's a very clinical atmosphere, almost as if it were a mock war being played on a map until one leaves this air-conditioned haven and goes back outside where it is 92 degrees today.

During the meeting, General Ewell (who I later learned had been nicknamed the "Butcher of the Delta") railed against his officers because we were losing the battle of the metrics. He slammed his pointer against the screen on which the projector displayed the latest scorecard. The 9th's body count was slipping below that of the other combat divisions in Vietnam. At that point, I recall he suggested counting the arms and legs separately the next time we swept a village.

The other metrics on the scorecard intrigued me. One was medals awarded. The other was time to conviction for those accused of crimes. I knew that the policy of awarding three bronze stars and two Army Commendation medals had me holding ceremonies every week. What I had not known was that awarding medals was a central strategy in boosting morale among the troops. I knew, in fact, that it did just the opposite. Losing self-respect for fighting in a war that made no sense was causing *low* morale, and receiving undeserved medals for fighting in an immoral war only made it worse.

Stressing time to conviction rather than time to trial was a tactic aimed at removing troublemakers as quickly as possible. That I expedited the special courts-martial in my battalion, often at the expense of the rights of the accused, really did not bother me much until later in life when thinking about my experience. That Vietnam veterans tended to keep their feelings on the war buried is widely known and true for me. But each of us has probably had something trigger those feelings much later in life, something different for each of us—a noise, a trip to the Wall, a smell, or something we read, as was the case with me.

The obituary of my commanding general, Julian J. Ewell, in the August 5, 2009, *Washington Post* ripped the last shreds of honor from my heart and brought me to tears. It began benignly enough, citing the impressive number of claimed enemy killed by the 9th Division during Operation Speedy Express:

> Under his command between December 1968 and May 1969, the 9th Infantry Division launched a large-scale offensive, Operation Speedy Express, that aimed to quickly eliminate enemy troops with overwhelming force. The division claimed that 10,899 enemies were killed during the operation, but only 748 weapons were seized—a disparity, investigators said, that could indicate that not all the dead were combatants.

Queasiness rose in my stomach, bile in my throat, as I read further...

> The army inspector general had written in 1972: "While there appears to be no means of determining the precise number of civilian casualties incurred by US forces during Operation Speedy Express, the extent of these casualties was indeed substantial, and that a fairly solid case can be constructed to show that civilian casualties may have amounted to several thousand (between 5,000 and 7,000)."

That report had been recently revealed by journalists Deborah Nelson and Nick Turse, who reported in 2008 that the vast scale of civilian deaths was the equivalent of "a My Lai a month." My Lai, the massacre of nearly 500 Vietnamese by American troops in 1968, had scandalized the nation, deeply embarrassed the army, and undercut support for the war.

Turse described Gen. Ewell's Delta operation in a December article in The Nation magazine. And in her book, *The War Behind Me* (2008), Nelson noted that after the operation ended and Gen. Ewell was at II Field Force, he "took notice of the civilian killings" and issued an order that such deaths would not be tolerated. Quoting Nick Turse, Nelson writes:

"From my research, the bulk of the evidence suggests that Julian Ewell presided over an atrocity of astonishing proportions," Turse said in an interview. "The Army had a lot of indications that something extremely dark went on down in the Delta from a variety of sources, but it opted not to vigorously pursue the allegations."

For the genocidal operation, Ewell was promoted by General Abrams to the next highest rank. After the Inspector General determined that the 9th killed between 5,000 and 7,000 unarmed civilians, as Burns laments in his tour de force production, "No one was ever held accountable." Oh, yes, they were. Each and every one of us who participated will live with the guilt of what we did the rest of our lives. That General Ewell was eulogized as a hero after he died is an atrocity in itself.

I felt like I had been punched in the stomach, hard. My breath left me as I thought, my god, I participated in a genocide of enormous proportions. I had attended one of the many meetings during which the massacres were ordered. Because the combat I saw was from the berm around the base, to my knowledge I never shot at a civilian. But in truth, we never knew if the shadows we fired at were combatants or a mama-san lost while trying to find a latrine at night.

As March slowly unfolded, the bombardment increased, as I wrote to Betsy.

We're still getting mortared quite regularly. Today I was in the pool at 12:30 when the sirens went off and we had to scramble for the bunker. Last night, we spent two hours in the bunker from 12:30 to 2:30 and still had to get up for work. We're still on yellow alert tonight, so I expect to be rousted out sometime. Yes, it does get on one's nerves. 135 days to R&R!!!

The next day's letter included this passage: "We were hit last night for the fifth or sixth night in a row and spent a delightful 2½ hours in the bunker. I now carry a good book along with my rifle and flak jacket." I cautioned her, "According to the experts, whoever they are, the VC are in the third and final stage of their new offensive. I'll be glad when it's over, as everyone is in vile moods from lack of sleep and jumpy nerves. Oh, what I would give for a big fat reassuring hug from my fragrant soft wife."

The next night, March 25th, I wrote during my shift on the berm:

The mosquitoes are too much out here tonight. They're huge and it's too hot to roll the sleeves down. We had a great battle in front of us about 1 mile out. Five helicopters were bombing the ground with rockets and other weapons. It resembled a bunch of Indians (helicopters) circling a wagon train (the VC). I'm glad the VC don't have any helicopters. That's the best weapon we have, if you can call weapons good.

I worked all the next day after an hour or so of sleep and returned to a night of berm duty, one of the worst for Dong Tam. As I described it to Betsy:

Last night will be imprinted on my mind for as long as I live. The VC hit the main ammo bunker…and the resulting explosion almost flattened Dong Tam. Out on the berm where I was sector duty officer, we had VC in front of us but never saw them, although we sure stayed awake looking. Anyway, we saw the rocket take off from the jungle and land on the other side of the camp. All of a sudden, this big cloud rose, and the earth started shaking, and then the concussion hit and I fell flat on my ass just from the concussion even though the explosion was three-quarters of a mile away. Our BOQ is a little closer by half a mile, and although the outside was not hurt, the explosion caused all the lockers to fall, along with all the dirt from the roof. When I got back from duty, my stuff was strewn all over the floor, as I have a shelf on the wall that came off, spilling everything on it. The good thing is I took everything out of the room, cleaned it, and neatly replaced it, so now my room looks so neat you'd never guess that old slobby Burton lived there. You've probably read about this incident in the papers already so it's not news. Why the hell do men fight wars and strive to invent better ways of killing each other? How stupid.

AP report on explosion that rocked Dong Tam

When I see an explosion like that one, I think men have bitten off more than they can chew. It looked like a small atom bomb going off. But I rallied my men and kept them alert so that the night passed without further incident. But that one blast moved one of our motor pool buildings off its foundation and bent the walls of the HQ.

...So much for the seriousness; on the funnier side, our officers'
lounge took a bad beating but rallied back to open tonight in the
highest traditions of the army. I'm back to my status as both the
adjutant and HQ detachment commander, so tonight I will be
safely bunkered away and out of harm's way.

What I omitted from my report to Betsy on the ammo dump explosion was the conversation I had with our operations center shortly after the
devastating blast. From the earpiece in my field phone, a voice screamed,
"Gas!" That warning required all in earshot to don their protective masks
because poison was in the air. "The VC don't have gas," I yelled back. "It's
not theirs, it's ours!" came the response. To this day, I have no idea what gas
was spewing into the air from our ammo dump. The prime suspect was the
tear gas we used to root VC from tunnels underground. But we were never
told, and no one dared to ask.

In that same letter, I also wrote about why an audio tape we were
exchanging would be delayed: "I was going to send you a tape tonight,
but our own artillery is sounding off and it might scare you. One gets
used to them after a while, so you hardly pay any attention to them. I
will tape to you tomorrow, although I would like to wait for your tape so
I can, in a very far-fetched sense, have a conversation with you. I want
that so much."

During this time, Betsy wrote me an angry letter. She had seen the
article in the *Boston Globe* and castigated me for not telling her the full
truth of the level of combat. She said she would rather know the truth
about the danger level than have me sugar-coat it. My letters did become
more descriptive after that.

I kept my own spirits up, as did my men, not just by counting the
days, but the hours, minutes, and seconds. It was not uncommon to get that
tight a time when I asked one of my men how "short" he was. For Betsy,
I counted, "131 long days until reunion and 265 until no more army—
at least the end is in sight. Must bed down now in my freshly made bed
(one bottom sheet slightly twisted with 2,000,000 wrinkles), as I am weary
from lack of sleep and lonely from lack of wife..."

The obsession with time left until the end of one's tour affected performance. One night as I walked behind the berm to ensure no breaks had
been made by incoming mortars, I found two of my men huddled in a shell

crater. I asked what they were doing there, since they were supposed to be out front at a listening post. "Please, sir," one of the kids pleaded, "don't send me out there. I've got two days and a wake-up left." I angrily pointed out that our defense relied on accurate reports from our listening posts to warn of infiltrating enemy. Also, knowing where they were supposed to be, we had withheld our fire thinking they were out there.

I relented, though, my harsher side giving over to empathy. "Go back to your unit and tell your first sergeant you have my permission to be replaced."

On another occasion, I was not as understanding. During that day, I had somehow acquired an affliction that raised my body temperature to 105 degrees. I had staggered over to the hospital, where the medic gave me a bottle of aspirin and told me to lie down in one of the upper bunks until the fever broke.

As I lay there shivering, I heard a call come over the field radio. "Bunker seven just took a direct hit on the roof! There's bodies everywhere. Get medics here fast!"

The two medics below me as I looked down from my upper bunk cast worried looks at each other. One of them said, "I'm not going out there. I'm short!"

With that, I rolled over to the side of the bunk, grabbed him by the collar, and yelled right in his ear, "Those are my men out there! Get your ass in the ambulance and go there now or I'll have you court-martialed and you'll never go home!"

Later, I heard that medic's voice reporting that they were coming into the hospital with a full load of wounded and asking that the operating room be readied.

When feeling sorry for myself, I had plenty of sad stories worse than mine to make me feel relatively well off. Take Specialist Fourth Class Blake, for example:

You want to hear a sad story? (I wrote Betsy). "This is about Spec 4 Blake of A Company. Blake extended over here (volunteered to stay 18 months), and because of this was entitled to take a 30-day leave. So Blake packs all his stuff and goes up to Tan Son Nhut air base to wait for his flight to Australia. After waiting a while, Blake decides that it would be more fun to stay in Saigon for a month shacked up with a gook. So he found a willing girl and thought he had it made. Anyway, Saigon is off limits to all members of the fighting 9th Division, so while Blake is out getting some more booze on his second day, the MPs picked him up and threw him in jail for two days. Now the MPs wouldn't let Blake back into the house where he was staying with the girl, so he does not know what happened to all his clothes, $400 in cash, and most of all, what happened to his rifle—which the girl took off with, obviously to sell to the VC.

Now when Blake gets back to Dong Tam, his CO gave him an Article 15 for being in an off-limits area, demotes him to a PFC, and fines him $100. Not only that, but come to find out that Blake caught the "clap" while shacked up and is now held for medical reasons so he can't take his leave. The troopies can really get themselves in some great predicaments.

Some of my men did not deserve the predicaments they faced. I gave one a compassionate leave because his wife had moved in with another man at home.

Sad story for the day is the guy I told you about before who went home on emergency leave because his wife had moved in with another man. He's back, and as it turned out, his wife was two months pregnant by this other guy, and while he was there, one of his three kids got sick and had to go the hospital. To do this, he had to try for an extension on his leave. He tried to get this, but somebody at division disapproved it, so the man was late to his flight and the government is making him pay the $200 for the flight [because] he was late. Stupid f---ing army. Anyway, I'm going to do my damndest to see if I can get his money back.

CHAPTER 8: THE INVITATION

You know, I can't help but feel discouraged about all this campus disorder stuff. That's big news now and is really depressing. Why can't
they just get blasted and go crazy on Saturday nights like we used to
do and let the establishment take care of themselves…

I received an A on my latest business test, so looking good for
a big ace. I'll be glad when it's over, though. It's a little too much. I
almost fell asleep tonight. The only thing that kept me awake was
our mortars, which are located right behind the classroom. It seems
so funny to sit in a class of learning while artillery is going off.
—Letter to my wife, May 12, 1969

Not that I thought about it much, but when I volunteered to serve in
Vietnam and might have died there, it would have been in the service
of my country, protecting our democracy as all my war heroes had done. I
never anticipated that some of my closest brushes with death would happen on Highway 4 connecting Dong Tam with Saigon while fulfilling
my mission of producing engraved invitations to my battalion commander's change-of-command ceremony. Glory, deserved or not, advanced the
interests of those regular army officers, especially as they sought promotion into the upper field-grade ranks and choice assignments. Ceremonies
offered a chance to garner false glory.

Thus I was not surprised when my CO called me into his office in
early May and handed me the invitation his counterpart in the 101st Air-
borne Division had sent him to *his* change-of-command ceremony. The
three-by-five high-quality paper emphasized the beauty of the multicol-
ored eagle embossed thereon with the shield and logo of America's most
famous paratrooper division.

"I want invitations to my change-of-command ceremony to look like or be nicer than this one," he ordered.

A call to my counterpart at the 101st gave me the name and address of the printer in Saigon where theirs had been done. He warned that the proof had to be developed at the company in Saigon, and I should watch them like a hawk to ensure it was done right and on time. While I did not mind breaking away for a day or two, driving to Saigon up Highway 4 could be treacherous, if not deadly. While we generally controlled the countryside during the days, the Viet Cong and NVA ruled the nights. But even during the day, our troops conducted raids, and generally hunted the enemy day and night, and I expected to see action as we traveled the 40 miles connecting the two points. I also knew that our mine sweepers did their work early in the mornings to clear the road of mines that the VC planted at night, but they could miss a few. So we had to guard against the possibility of running over one and dying from the explosion.

On May 3, 1969, along with three of my men, one on the .50-caliber machine gun mounted on my jeep and his armed friend next to him in the backseat, and me sitting next to the driver in front—helmet, flak jacket, loaded M-16 off safety and all—we departed early for Saigon. Luckily, we hit no mines and only heard sporadic gunfire not aimed our way except for a couple of sniper rounds that whizzed by above our heads. At one point we passed through a village on the dusty dirt road. In the town's center, we spied a pile of bodies in peasant clothes; we did not stop to inspect.

My letter that day to Betsy reported why we failed to accomplish our mission on that run:

> I'm all sunburned to a crisp. We went up to Saigon today in an open jeep, and as it turned out, it was 100 degrees most of the day and the sun really beat down on my fat head. On top of that, we got lost in Saigon and didn't find the place we were looking for until about 3:30. We were looking for the gook printer who is going to print up the invites to the change-of-command ceremony. When we got there, the guy that handles that stuff had gone for the day. Yeah, I was a mite perturbed. So we crashed and banged and screeched our way out of the morass of traffic Saigon is and

made it back tonight at 5:30 without incident. Oh, by the way, it rained this morning, not too hard but identifiable as rain. This is the first time in 6 months and marks the start of the season.

On May 5th, I complained of my second try. "I took another day trip to Saigon today just to order these damn invitations. The truck we went in had no glass in the window on my side, so I am now sporting a severe windburn and a bad case of nerves from riding in Saigon. Rome would seem like a kiddy-car track compared to that." What irked me most about risking my life for engraved invitations that day was losing study time for the business course I had enrolled in through the University of Maryland at Dong Tam. A West Point graduate who also held an MBA taught the course in an underground bunker. He tried to time our class breaks with mortar attacks so we could duck into the safest part of the sandbag-walled edifice. But sometimes he just kept going.

This being the first course after being married and being taken seriously by myself, I griped to Betsy, "I'm getting a lot out of this course, but I'll be glad when it's over—like today I had to try and read while driving to Saigon. The only time I got out of the truck was when I went into the printer's office. I think I will concentrate on my job and relax my two off hours at night. Of course, in my idle time, all I think about is you."

Two weeks later, I planned to finish this project, but that was not to be.

Today was a rather frustrating day. I was supposed to go to Saigon this morning to pick up the final copies of the invitations I have been trying to get out. The jeep was late, and I arrived one minute before this printing plant closed. I ran into the little guy who runs the place, and he informed me that mine were done except for the orange coloring in the unit crest. So now I must go back and pick them up Tuesday. Then I went over to Tan Son Nhut to get the watch we got for my colonel engraved. The gook there said he couldn't do it as the vise he had would injure the watch. I did get some new shower clogs and a Time magazine though. They have some stylish clothes up there also. I think I might get a rather wild going-on-R&R outfit—be prepared. To top it all off, the driver I was given was so terrible I finally relieved him. This kid had never driven a stick except for a few times, and he was trying to drive me around Saigon where experienced drivers go insane. I am completely hoarse from yelling at him. You would have been proud of my yelling, dear—I sounded like you when you get pissed at me sometimes. So I returned empty-handed, but it was a day away from the office and a respite.

Betsy's response to the invitation episode—words like "I can't believe I could lose you to a fancy invitation"—caused me to mention the incident no more. I did get the final copies (in yet another trip), which went out with great fanfare, though few showed up for the event. But that wasn't the point: showing off what he could do (or get his staff to do) *was*.

More than risking my life for invitations wore on me in late March early April. Though the assaults tapered off somewhat, I got my first sleep in three days on March 27th. Then the monsoon season overcame us with 103-degree average temperatures and the heaviest downpours I had ever experienced. One of our trucks hit a guy wire, bringing down the largest antenna we had. That night a colonel arrived to inspect the damage and demanded a room in my BOQ. So I had to "roust people out to get a room fixed up," but he complained of no lights. I explained the huge explosion during the big blast attack had broken all the light bulbs.

Reports of the big explosion troubled me, as I began realizing that the war of attrition had a rationale in that the rockets and mortars were launched from nearby villages and hamlets. These became worthy targets for our artillery and no doubt added to the enemy as well as civilian body count the 9th was piling up.

Major Jim tried to cheer us up through food and spiritual sustenance. "We're having a pancake breakfast Easter morning in our lounge (Major Jim's idea). He became a 90-day-less today and is now officially considered short. After the breakfast, I'm going to church and say a few words for you and me."

Encouraged and feeling guilty, I wandered toward the chapel, as did other soldiers presenting quizzical countenances. I wondered if they, like me, prayed from time to time when the mortars hit nearby that the next one would not land on them as they tried to crawl into their helmets. As I came close, I noticed that the congregation spilled out into the bare dirt acre away from any buildings that could attract incoming enemy rounds. I did approach the base chapel but stopped short of participating.

No benevolent god, I decided, would countenance the mayhem besetting our base and the region around it. I went to the pool and had a refreshing swim instead.

The ammo dump explosion weighed heavily on my mind at that time. As I described to Betsy on April 6th:

> Nobody was killed in the [battalion] fortunately. A few guys were shaken up quite a bit. Major Caddigan was all soaped up in the shower when it went off and ran for the bunker that is right out-side. He tripped and fell in the dirt, so there he was for the rest of the evening with a towel, and covered with soap and dirt. I'm sending the clippings my Ma sent me from the Boston papers. Five hundred tons of ammo went up and just flattened every-thing within 200 yards of the area. All night long and through-out the next day, ammo was still going off, as no one could get close enough to put the fire out. But by the next afternoon, all the ammo had been replaced by air and the artillery on Dong Tam was blasting away in full fury to show Charlie that he hadn't done us a damaging blow. (Flags wave–band plays–big deal–I want to go home.)

My commanding officer must have been worried about me, though, as he reassured me that he very much liked my work. No doubt that was in large part the result of the personal medals and unit citation I had copped for him and his unit. Looking back, he may also have worried that my having no interest in a military career meant I could not be influenced by threats of withholding praise or desires to get it, which burned in the breasts of the "lifers" in our unit. They were mostly good people and skilled leaders. But the motivation to look good, not save our country, affected their behavior and performance.

Early in April, I was assured I could keep the job of adjutant, which I liked. As I explained to Betsy:

> Colonel talked with me today and was worried that I would insist on getting changed from my present job as adjutant. Most of the career officers are worried about getting command time, and I told him I was not staying in and liked the experience I was getting

and would stay as adjutant the whole time. No adjutant has lasted over three months in the battalion because of the strain, etc., but it doesn't bother me. My colonel told me he really liked having me as adjutant and wanted me to stay on because of my sense of humor, which keeps him loose. Naturally, I blushed because I hate compliments so much, but actually it was sort of gratifying, as I am a man of sometimes high temper and now seem to have it under control when the strain is applied.

My frame of mind remained strong though under siege. On April first, I told Betsy of a more intense encounter.

A Lieutenant came in to see me today crying, literally about what a bastard his CO was. I agreed with him on some points. He's just a dumb indoctrinated jerk beyond hope [describing the company commander]. I tried to explain this to the kid, but he kept crying, which was very disconcerting. I've never seen so many grown men cry in my life. When the pressure gets heavy, it seems to be the thing to do. Having lived with pressure most of my army career, it doesn't faze me too much, and besides, my days are numbered in the *ahhhmy*.

That leaders must be ready to shoulder the emotional problems of others constituted a valuable lesson for me as a twenty-five-year-old. Later, as an academic dean and for thirteen years a college president, the Vietnam experience helped me retain my own emotional strength while dealing with the life problems of over a thousand employees. I will never know if I would have developed this trait had I not gone to war. But there must be a better way.

Jim Caddigan was a big help, though. He even gave me a nickname that stuck and made me feel good. Betsy did not like that I was called "Bat," but I liked it. "Now looking at your letter of the 5th, which states you don't like the nickname Bat. Well, it came from Major Caddigan when I walked into the bunker one night during an alert with a black hip holster and loaded .45 like Bat Masterson. He called me Bat and so it goes."

CHAPTER 9: NO ANESTHESIA

Mid-May brought a mild cessation in mortar and rocket attacks on Dong Tam, though two of the worst incidents for me were yet to come. One salutary effect of taking college courses in a war zone had our instructor often "…letting us out early due to the alert status tonight." We had been warned of a major attack the night before that did not materialize and suspected that the one predicted for this night would "never come off." I did note in passing, "It's a very murky, sinister night out. The temperature is still around 90 degrees with high humidity."

Apparently, my instincts were right, and that night passed peacefully. The next morning, "I made my last trip to Saigon and procured my invitations, so that mission is accomplished. I'm glad I won't have to make that trip again." I did make several more trips up Highway 4 to Long Binh "to hand carry some orders through so my colonel can get his awards the day of the ceremony." Getting out of the line of fire on base—even though danger lurked on the road—was therapeutic. That night I marveled that "The sky is full of millions of crinkly lightning, as it's going to storm soon." I had planned to study for the final into the wee hours to get a good grade, something I had failed to do during my previous years in school and college. But it turned out the enemy had other ideas.

The next day I mourned, "I tried to study last night, but we were mortared…fairly steadily. Jim Coleman was duty officer on the berm last night when a rocket came and landed on the road beside the bunker. The thing was a dud, but Jim was a white Negro for quite a while." He and I had a long talk about the meaning of life and the meaning of survival as I tried to calm him down. Most of the rocket-propelled grenades (RPGs) detonate. Perhaps it was then that Jim decided to abandon his career military plans and opt for law school and a career as a civil rights advocate.

We did talk about our close calls. On a previous occasion, I had exited my jeep and walked around the blast wall guarding the door to my command bunker when a mortar round landed near the vehicle outside. The explosion destroyed the jeep and would have turned me to pulp if I had stopped to tie my boot or blow my nose; anything costing me even a few seconds could have ended my life.

My only "injury" was truly self-inflicted, as I confessed to Betsy on May 14th: "We got hit again last night with three rounds landing in the battalion area. Only one guy from this battalion was hurt (not seriously). I sprained a finger in the scramble to get out of the HQ building when the rounds started coming in. I did it pushing a slowpoke out of the way while heading for the door. That's your hero husband for you." Apparently, Betsy picked up on that story, because on May 27th, I elaborated, "Yes, I really got my finger sprained pushing someone out of the way. I think he fell in front of me—but it's everyone for himself when those rounds start coming in." Later in that letter, after telling her that Major Jim, very pleased with my performance, did not understand "why I'm so STRAC [militarily straight] yet don't like the army. I find it's a lot easier to work with no pressure whatsoever. My bosses both realize I'm getting out, and any pressure of efficiency reports, etc., don't mean a thing to me." Major Jim, in fact, gave me a 98 out of 100 on my Officer Efficiency Report, the highest by far of all the captains in the battalion.

Perhaps this experience contributed to the leadership philosophy I often articulated to my staff when in leadership positions in higher education. I suggested it was the role of leaders to create an environment in which organization members felt respected and valued. In a P.S. to that letter, I also noted presciently, "War seems to have calmed down—I still don't see peace for another couple of years. Every time we let up, they come right back. The biggest mess in the history of the world."

What I did not know then, though the incessant ringing in my ears should have forewarned me, is that the damage being done to my hearing (which eventually led to the VA-supplied electronic devices that serve me well now) began on the berm at Dong Tam. As described to Betsy on June 15th, "Berm duty went nicely last night. The only trouble is an artillery battery set up right behind the command post where we sit all night long, *Boom, Boom, Boom*—deafening." At times I recall the concussion from the 155mm howitzer, if fired as I walked by the muzzle, caused the bells to ring in my head and cost me any hearing for an hour or so. People now wear ear protection running lawn mowers; we had none for when the most powerful cannons in our arsenal sent projectiles so far, we could not hear them land.

Our worse loss did not come from enemy fire. As I tell Betsy in my letter of June 13th, "Very shocking thing today—a guy from a signal detachment next door to us committed suicide by blowing himself up with a hand grenade. Unfortunately, there were six other people around him, and three of them were killed. I was the first to reach the scene, as I was in the outhouse not far from there. I will never forget that scene as long as I live. I tried to help one of the wounded, but he was pretty bad. A Vietnamese woman was hurt also."

That day, while I was using the outhouse near a cleared area where we cleaned weapons, a tremendous explosion knocked me out the door and onto the ground. The siren warning of incoming rounds sounded immediately, and I ran around to the site of the detonation to give aid to the wounded. The scene confronting me stopped me cold. Body parts were scattered around a smoking black crater where the table had stood at which soldiers had been cleaning their weapons after a night repelling attacks on the berm. A witness later testified that one of the men had reached into the case of live hand grenades on the table, pulled the pin releasing the clip, and replaced it in the partially full box. The grenade and box detonated almost simultaneously.

I heard a sigh to my right and turned to render aid, perhaps to clear the man's airway as we'd been trained to do for anyone having trouble breathing. But the smoking torso from which the air escaped had no head or arms or legs. I froze in shock. I knew I should move but could not. Some of my men arrived about then, picked me up by the arms, and walked me to the shower, which I took fully clothed to remove the human offal clinging to me and my uniform. Apparently, I had tried to uncover the living beneath what was left of the bodies of the men standing closest to the blast.

It now seems a bit insensitive, but in the same letter, I spoke about R&R plans, the fact that my birthday present hadn't arrived, and the count of days left until I would meet Betsy in Hawaii halfway through my tour. I closed the letter with, "Tomorrow night is berm duty night, so I will be spending the evening out there. We have been getting hit fairly regularly lately, so out on the berm is safe [because] the rounds usually fall inside the compound. Major Caddigan moved his bunk into the bunker today and will probably live there for the rest of his tour (9 days)."

I believe it was around this incident that I wrestled with the issue of what to tell family members when one of our men died of friendly fire, a drug overdose, or, as in this case, suicide. The standard letter failed to distinguish, stating generically, "I regret to inform you that your son [fill in the blank] died in the service of his country during combat operations in the Republic of South Vietnam." Army regulations required this letter and none other.

One night, though, I drafted another: "I regret to inform you that your son [fill in the name] died needlessly by his own hand from his depression from fighting in a war he could not comprehend, and we should not be fighting." I kept this letter in my desk unsent. But more than once, I thought about using it when death came by such circumstances.

Fortunately, in a way, I had little time to be depressed. With a new CO and EO arriving, I spent much of my time preparing briefings and dealing with the anxieties of executing the military rituals to perfection that had to go on even in a combat area. Describing my dilemma to Betsy on May 31st, I complained, "Things are getting a little screwed up around here, as SFC Johnson is going on leave to Sydney, Australia, tomorrow, and the guy that stands in for him didn't show up for work today as he drank all night and half the morning. I have to get a 24-page document out in the next two days, and everything is confused by a change-of-command ceremony thrown in the middle. Blewy!!! Tonight, I have berm duty, and tomorrow I must arrange a seating plan for all the brass at the ceremony. 75 DAYS TO R&R."

The battalion NCOs threw a party for my colonel that night. "Our Sergeant Major is Hawaiian. Yesterday, they went out and bought a pig from the Viets, and last night they shot and butchered it (after it was inspected by the vet). Tonight is the party and the pig is still roasting on the spit. I will miss the party, as I have duty tonight. I really won't miss it much, though, as I'm getting sick of talking to drunken NCOs."

Some good news buoyed me through this period, however. I did get an A in the course I took, one of my first ever post-high school. And on May 27th, I received my acceptance letter to the MBA program at UNH. While the army would make it impossible to begin in the fall of 1969 because I had to fulfill three full years as part of my agreement, I could defer my admission to the fall of 1970. Being able to see a trajectory into the future kept my spirits up even as I more and more questioned our being in Vietnam.

The schizophrenia induced by reducing the Vietnamese to gooks we could fire at, at will, off the berm while getting to know, admire, and even have great affection for some of the people I worked with was hard to accommodate in one brain and one heart. I spent a long afternoon at the orphanage in My Tho one Sunday learning the history of the area through the eyes of the wonderfully kind leaders at the orphanage, members of a French order of nuns. As I relate to Betsy in my letter of May 25th, "I went to the orphanage to deliver all the packages of clothing that have been sent by my mother. I sat and talked with the Mother Superior, Sister Amelia, and her right-hand nun, Sister Joseph, who is a real character. She has no teeth and speaks real good English. She gave me the whole history of the orphanage, which started in 1816. Later, I had the unfortunate experience of seeing a leper colony, which made me physically ill."

On June 3rd, I sent Betsy pictures of my visit, including the lepers who lived at the facility. As I described the pictures, "They are Vietnamese. Sister George is about 4'3" tall. I didn't throw up at the time when I saw the lepers, but I can tell you—prepare yourself—they were picking scabs while I was watching them."

In Vietnam, facilities such as the My Tho Orphanage served many types of people: orphans, the intellectually impaired, lepers, and others no one else would care for. To my knowledge, the place received no governmental support and was run solely by the nuns. That they became so dependent on us would be an enormous problem for me a little later.

On June 2nd, we held a formal military dinner in the mess tent, which I described to Betsy as follows:

Today is the morning after the night before. We had my colonel's military dinner last night and he cried. He is really a dedicated man. Later, back at the lounge, he took each officer aside and personally thanked him. When he took me aside, I told him that most of the time I hated his guts but respected him. He thought that was good, as he said he pushed everyone to do their best and he got it. He's an amazing man. I'm enclosing the program and the prayer I wrote for the occasion. Not bad for a sporadic Christian. One more event to go—the ceremony itself—and all this will be over. Meantime, I notice I have but 72 days to H-day. Short! I now have to put little place cards on the chairs of all the guests, so our guides will put them in the right order—woe to me if some full bird gets seated amongst majors."

Later in the evening, after we'd been drinking for quite a while, my colonel and I had an argument about the things concerning me: the focus on awards, officers' privilege, risking my life to get engraved invitations, and so on. At one point, he became very angry at me and I reached for my .45. At that point, we both realized we had better calm down, turn away, and head to our own hooches.

Major Caddigan leads ceremony flanked by the author
and Captains Griese and Coleman, Dong Tam, May 1969

The next day, I wrote Betsy, "Your pictures couldn't have come at a better time…as all the ceremonies and protocol went off in a flawless manner. I went to the helipad and waved good-bye to my colonel, which ended the pressure to get everything done on time. I am beat physically and mentally tonight, as is most everybody. I have decided not to take the next course, as it did cause a lot of work during the last one, and I know that we will be doing a lot of new things [that] the new CO will want."

The new commanding officer came less wired than his predecessor. He expanded lunch hour to an hour and a half, among other things. My life would become less busy. The enemy cooperated by delivering no assaults during the week of June 4th, a trend I hoped would continue for the balance of my tour. But that was not to be.

"I had an early birthday party today, as my mother sent me a cake, actually a large brownie, with lettering and everything. Jim Coleman and Jim Caddigan came by and we had orange soda and cake. They toasted my 25th and wished me many more. The promotion party last night was interrupted by a mortar attack, which destroyed the main officers' club and injured 11 people. After the attack, we returned to the lounge and finished the party."

My early birthday present came from President Richard Nixon when he announced, as I wrote to Betsy, that he wanted "…to bring [home] 5% of the Vietnam warriors." Rumors swirled, and the betting was that a full division would be deactivated. Since the 9th Division had been created and deployed to "pacify" the Mekong Delta, with the advertised mission accomplished, according to Washington, we began hearing rumors that we might be chosen.

Apparently, the VC and NVA in our area failed to believe that rumor. Instead, combat increased, not decreased as one would have hoped, given the news. A week or so later, I experienced a personal incident forever indelible in my memory.

"Lothrop's been hit!" one of my men screamed into my field phone as I walked the area on June 13st, checking my men during a mortar attack.

"Where is he?" I asked.

"He was in the shower when a mortar came through the roof and detonated, spraying him with shrapnel, sir. He's a mess."

Specialist 5 Kenny Lothrop was a great kid. Out of Ohio with some college behind him, I had made him our supply clerk, a critical position that he filled well. Plus, we had become personal friends because Kenny often stayed late to help me out in the headquarters. "Get him to the hospital and I'll meet you there," I ordered.

When I arrived at the 9th Division Field Hospital a few buildings down from our headquarters, a scene out of hell stopped me in my tracks. We had taken heavy losses. The dead were stacked on the right side of the corridor leading to the one working operating room; the wounded were piled up on the left side. I spotted one of my men and yelled, "Where's Lothrop?"

"Under here someplace," he said as we began flipping through the wounded pile. We could do him no good if he were in the other one.

Finally, I found him on the bottom, turning blue but with no sign of blood on his front side though his breathing was badly labored. Turning him over, I found the wound, a gaping gash in his back, which told me that a piece of shrapnel had entered his body but not exited.

"Pick him up and get him to the operating room," I directed while pushing my way there to prepare for his medical attention. As I entered the room, a young doctor with blood on his arms up to his elbows eyed Lothrop as my men carried him into the operating room, one on each of his corners.

The doctor rolled the body of the man he had been working on, but who was apparently dead, off the table onto a waiting stretcher. The man would fight no more. Then, probing the wound on Lothrop's back after we hoisted him onto the stainless-steel table bearing the blood spatters from several wounded before him, the doctor quavered, "Hold him down. I have to operate and there's no time for anesthesia."

I lay across Lothrop's chest while my men held down his feet and arms. Lothrop was not particularly tall at 5'8" or so, but he was a very solid 175–185 pounds with the body of someone who lifted weights.

Lothrop screamed as the doctor sliced open his chest, inserted a tube, and blew into it to inflate his collapsed lung.

After a while, Lothrop began breathing regularly, and the doctor ordered the orderlies to move him to a recovery area. As I wrote to Betsy the next morning:

> I spent the better part of last night with one of my men who was hit during a mortar attack on Dong Tam. I held him down while the doctor worked on him. There were other wounded in the hospital treatment area, as we had quite a few wounded. I tell you this in keeping with the policy of complete honesty on what is going

on. There were some people who were pretty bad off there, which led the thought to cross my mind that if people could see how senseless any fighting is, and what it does to humans, they would never fight again. My man is all right today, thank goodness, and I am much relieved. Some of the people I saw there last night did not fare as well. Don't worry about me—I'm the first one in the bunker.

On my third daily visit with Lothrop as he recuperated, I found him in his backless Johnny sitting on the sandbag wall outside the hospital. He clutched the stand with numerous bags hanging from it, some dripping through tubes and needles into veins in the crooks of his arms. He grinned at me broadly.

"What's so funny?" I asked.

"Sir," he announced, "I'm going home."

Tears streaked both of our cheeks. A good kid like Lothrop did not deserve to die for a lost cause. Yet he served his country to the best of his ability, a story retold frequently over the course of the Vietnam War.

Concerned that she would worry about my well-being, I wrote Betsy that night:

Not to leave you with such lugubrious thoughts, I now turn to the fact I will be home, or at least with you, about 3½ months early. My adventure is over, and my patriotic desires have been more than satisfied, and I am ready to return to a normal life of kids and wife. I thank you for your voluminous letter of 11th, as it was refreshing to say the least to hear of your adventures.

I am sure your letter of tomorrow will have all kinds of questions about whether or not I am coming home with the 9th. I will keep you posted of further developments.

The next night, I announced in my letter to her:

It's 7:00 on 14 June and we just had the message read to us from the commanding general saying that the 9th Division is going home except for one brigade. Now, this does not mean everyone in the division is going home. Those people [who] have a major portion of their time completed are going back. What a "major portion" is, is unknown yet. Everything is in a turmoil. It means a hell of a lot of work for me as the adjutant, believe me. I will keep you informed of what is going on. I don't know whether our R&R will be canceled or not. So, stay loose—that's all I can say.

Military order peaked at this point and waned significantly thereafter, which made the job of organizing the redeployment of our battalion highly problematic. My organizing and leadership skills were put to a significant test. My challenge became getting 600 soldiers who had been told we had won the war in the Delta—something few of us believed—to fully engage in their duties knowing that they would be leaving the country and the war in three months.

First things first, on June 19th, I paid tribute to the man who had made my job and my life so much easier, Jim Caddigan:

Tonight is Major Caddigan's last night on Dong Tam, and we are throwing a party for him. I made up a scrapbook with all his high points in them and added some humorous comments. I also designed a scroll for him, which will bear all the 9th Sig Bn officers' signatures on it. He is a nervous wreck now, as we have been mortared the first two nights. I think he plans to sleep in the bunker tonight.

The little bit at the bottom was just typed by Jim Caddigan himself. He hasn't seen his wife for a year, as R&R wasn't feasible due to his four kids. I wish him well.

So far, all instructions on the big MOVE have been verbal, and I will feel much better when I see myself on the orders for Hawaii. Then I will show you how I have shaped up, as you put it. I Love You!

Short-timer
SEE YA BETS!!!!!!! *(from Major Jim)*

CHAPTER 10: HAWAII

*The author welcomes Betsy to Hawaii
several days after the 9th Division landed there*

On June 20, 1969, I tried to write Betsy as to what would happen next. Rumors flew within the battalion as to who would go back and when. Celebratory pronouncements in the Stars and Stripes contrasted with the actuality on the ground in Dong Tam. "If you think this letter sounds confused, it is only indicative of my mind as everyone tries to comprehend what is happening," I wrote Betsy. "You would not believe the utter confusion everyone is in right now." I did close that letter with a poem, one of the few I've ever written. Betsy's favorite flower was the daisy, and it became my metaphor for her.

> *So the droop daisy can lift her head toward the sun once again*
> *for Daddy's coming home forever, and although it has been raining*
> *for two days straight (there goes my tan), the sun is shining*
> *in my heart once again as I will have my Betsy shortly.*

I Love You

The field-grade officers wanted nothing to do with a retreat. And those with partial tours wanted to complete the ones they were in to get full credit so they would not be sent back to the war. The career NCOs were in the same position and sought to transfer out before the redeployment, then two and a half months away. Compounding the dilemma of staffing for the redeployment was the "early out" program that allowed the lower-ranking enlisted men instant discharge when they returned to the States if they finished 13 months in country. Many of them sought to transfer out of the 9th before the division departed so they wouldn't miss the chance for an early separation. These forces made it problematic to get a complement of troops sufficient to look like a returning division when we hit Fort Lewis with the first redeployed unit and Schofield Barracks, Hawaii, for the rest of us. Maximum political effect, not ease of execution, drove the planning process.

The new battalion commander gave me total responsibility for this exercise. Compounding all of this was an inconvenient truth: our morning reports on our manpower were only marginally accurate. At some point in this time frame, a VC sapper blew up the division's computer center, destroying equipment on which manpower records were stored. We also knew that several men were simply unaccounted for.

Truth was, we were unsure what Americans were out there in the Delta and what they were doing. Apparently, with word getting out, stragglers began showing up outside our berm seeking sanctuary. I recall vividly a Green Beret walking toward my bunker with a weapon over his head. From that crossbow dangled the scalps of suspected VC sympathizers he had assassinated during the year or so he had been living off the land. I reported his arrival, and he was spirited off the base shortly thereafter.

Panicky colonels called me from Military Assistance Command (MACV) in Saigon asking for information because they were having difficulty making the numbers they needed. At the bottom of the information chain, there was little I could tell them. They had a political problem: the president had bragged about sending a successful division home, but that division was depleted of troops, never mind claims of success not matching with reality. An advertisement in the Vietnam edition of *Stars and Stripes* drew few responses. It was surreal that our president bragged about troops returning home and we were not able to find them.

Eventually, I received a call from MACV with the solution. A colonel informed me that prisoners in Long Bien Jail, the in-country prison, with a month or so left on their sentences, would be shipped to me for redeployment to the States. Cases of medals would come with them to make them look good. I was ordered to personally count them twice a day until we departed. They would not be armed. I remember pointing out to this faceless colonel that despite what Nixon bragged about at home, the VC continued to assault our base, more boldly now that they knew we had ceased our offensive operations. The 7th ARVN Division, our sister Vietnamese unit, took on more of a role as the 9th US Division prepared to leave. Relying on them for security left us uneasy, so we slept with our weapons (when sleep was something we had a chance to enjoy). As I recall, we were ordered to turn our weapons over to the ARVN troops, but not one of us did.

As I finished this book, through a friend I met with Mr. Tran (Trong) Nghia who had served in the ARVN, reaching the rank of colonel and appointed a district chief in a province near the one where I was. He reported that the 7th ARVN division we left behind had been able to hang on until the war ended in 1975. He complained that neither the American nor South Vietnamese soldiers received the "proper acknowledgment and respect they deserved." He said he indicated to then Vietnamese President Thieu, with whom he met once a month, that South Vietnam could not win the war. "The South Vietnamese were short on weapons and ammunition, which were cut by the American government at the last minute." Mr. Nghia accuses the US of pulling away abruptly, leaving behind the Vietnamese allies.

When the war ended with the signing of the Paris Peace Accords he asserts, "Right after the fall of Saigon, the South Vietnamese people and soldiers were treated brutally by the new government. Many soldiers and officers were tricked into reporting to the government only to be brought directly to the reeducation camps without knowledge of their families. Many died in these camps due to hard labor, torture, and mind games played by the communist government." It would be fourteen years in such a camp before Mr. Nghia would be released and reunited with his family. He now resides in Arizona.

Colonel Tran (Trong) Nghia. Army of the Republic of Vietnam

In our efforts to retrieve unaccounted-for troops, our men identified an American working in the NCO club on Dong Tam who was assigned to my battalion but had been listed as missing in action for many months. He had married a Vietnamese woman and was living in a village near the base. Following his arrest, while filling out the charge sheet, I came to the "maximum sentence" check box. The form offered two choices: check here if in time of peace; check there if at war. I asked Sergeant Johnson if we were at war in the legal sense. He did not know. I called the 9th Division Staff Judge Advocate's Office asking the same question. He had no clue either. Apparently, a message went all the way to the Pentagon seeking an answer,

Col Nghia; the author, Col Nghia's daughter Anhdao Tran Moseman

one of no small consequence. If at peace, the sentence was life imprisonment. If at war, death.

We huddled in a bunker some time later under red alert, enemy
mortar rounds landing nearby, when a message arrived from MACV. It
coldly advised that since Congress had never declared war, the maximum
sentence would be life imprisonment. We were not at war. Could have
fooled me. I announced the verdict to my troops as they fired their M-16s
at enemy shadows attempting to sneak close enough to blow us up. Extra
beers were consumed after I left duty that night.

Most clearly, a half century later, I recall with anguish one phone
conversation with a colonel at MACV. I had called to inquire how we
could get the orphans out when we left the area. "What are you talking
about?" he asked with agitation.

"For the past seven months, we have supported a large orphanage,
many of American parentage, in My Tho City. What will happen to them
when we leave?"

"Screw 'em!" he blurted. "Who cares?"

I did care—a lot. Of all the images waking me up at 4 a.m. now is
that little girl, Ho, the one who took my finger and walked with me as I
delivered clothes to the kids in the orphanage. I see her standing by the

gate the Sunday after we left. I wonder how long she watched the street we normally came down before realizing we were never coming back.

The author and Ho connect in one of the last times he saw her

On June 23, 1969, I received with my mother's letter containing the June 13, 1969, bulletin of the Payson Park Church in Belmont. It includes an explanatory note with a letter I wrote to them:

> Wayne Burton has spent his free time in Vietnam helping greatly at an orphanage. Clothes were donated to the orphanage from Mothers' Club rummage collection. Barbara Burton has mended and sent these clothes to her son—here is his reply:
> "I would like to express [the] gratitude of my men and myself for your generous donation of clothing to the My Tho Orphanage. Efforts such as this reaffirm our conviction that the American people are supporting us amid the controversy and criticism. One

tends to forget that the people who suffer during conflicts such as this are often the innocent, in this case children.

"I wish you all could witness the joy of seeing the children sporting 'new clothes.' I am happy to have witnessed it for you. You have not only made a compassionate, humanitarian gesture, but have helped the United States in its cause here by making friends. You have shown that Americans are kind and responsive to the needs of others. Once again, I express my gratitude and let you know you contributed greatly to a group of small Vietnamese orphans."

Wayne M. Burton

The deafness I live with from artillery and the memories of mangled bodies may diminish in time. Any PTSD the VA believes afflicts me now (50% PTSD) I believe arises from the betrayal of the people we said we would protect. I knew that many of the orphans had American fathers and would fare poorly as mixed-race people in Asian culture. But you heard my orders.

The redeployment continued apace, with the first group departing to great fanfare. As I describe to Betsy, though, not all was as it seemed.

I guess I should feel good to be a part of history, but I'd trade it all just to be with you. The berm was quiet last night, and it looks like the VC are going to let us go in peace (knock on wood). The first unit [that] is going back is coming in this weekend. Most of the guys going with it are short-timers who have been with other units. This particular battalion will be the publicity-getter and will be paraded in Saigon and Seattle to get the full political benefits, but between you and me, most of the guys never saw the unit before, as they are from other units. But practically everyone with over six months in country will get out of Vietnam, which is the most important thing. Again, between you and me, nobody including myself believes the Vietnamese can cope with the VC after we leave.

The last six weeks crawled by—minutes turned into hours, hours seemed like days. With little time remaining, I had 390 spaces to fill and

106 people to do it with. MACV's feverish work continued to produce a dribble of troops to go back. The VC continued to harass us, as I reported to Betsy: "We were hit three times last night but not very heavy. One guy brought a guitar into the bunker, and I tried to play it but flubbed badly and everyone booed and hissed. I must practice in Hawaii."

The next day we held another change-of-command ceremony, no invitations this time, as the lieutenant colonel taking us back to the world gave a "fire and brimstone speech, which we all yawned at," I conveyed to Betsy that night. "We've been through too many leaders to be impressed by rhetoric."

On July 16th, I acknowledged to Betsy "my 7th monthly anniversary in Vietnam, and I can say that I have more than fulfilled my patriotic spirit. I have no regrets about leaving, believe me. If nothing else, I can criticize this war with firsthand experience."

My circle of friends would make the diversity experts celebrate today. Tony Morano was a tough-talking, big-hearted guy from Brooklyn who "looked like a hood"; Jim Coleman, the African-American from Baltimore; Patrick Costales, a Hawaiian captain and "real cute guy"; and me. Pat had been awarded a Bronze Star for valor, and he deserved it. (I did not think I deserved the three Bronze Stars for achievement and two Army Commendation Medals awarded to me during that time. "I'm really not being modest when I say I've just done my job," I told Betsy.)

On August 8th, with a week to go, I reported to Betsy on a "wild day." "We held a muster in the motor pool and took 600 men and put them in groups they are supposed to be in for processing, finding out who was and who wasn't supposed to be there. Being troopies, of course, they were all dumb, and it made for an exasperating morning."

My attitude suffered during my last days in Vietnam, extending to my indifference to my hair length. My new CO, Colonel Loman, did not know what to make of me. He was "upset because my hair [was] getting long," I bragged to Betsy. By the time I mustered out in October, it was over my collar. I'm not sure why—perhaps a subconscious act of insubordination? Who knows? But being indispensable at that point, the only officer with a handle on the situation and no aspirations to a career, I could not have cared less.

That wild day continued busy however, as I conducted two court-martials with crime rampant. I also held a huge award ceremony as the 9th sought to look as glorious as possible when we hit US soil.

On August 14th, I wrote Betsy:

Dear Sunflower, I'm sitting here completely naked, shining my boots and staring at the calendar. Four days and a wake-up!! Tomorrow is muster day on Dong Tam as we round up everyone on the base and find out where they belong—should be interesting. We also must count heads and make sure we have enough to go to Hawaii (333). Sunday, we turn in our suitcases, and we live out of a kit bag for two days. Monday, we must turn in our beds and sleep on the floor so that after we leave the area will be completely clean. We had to close our club tonight to clean it out. We had a last beer and a toast and locked it up. Sort of sad! That dirty old place was the only bright spot in the area. We showed a delightful movie called *Wild on the Streets*, which is sort of depressing. I then had three hours of meetings tonight, trying to figure out who's where. More depressing! I still see names and numbers in my sleep. I know—I volunteered. Well, I'm un-volunteering Tuesday. I love you and still miss you even with the nearness of our reunion.

Three days later, I wrote my last letter from Vietnam:

You will probably be able to sit and look at me while you're reading this—or at least you will have talked with me on the phone. Today we turn in our luggage, which will go in the belly of the plane. Of course, there is much excitement and confusion. Yesterday, we lined everyone up in the motor pool and I gave them their flight numbers. We are traveling by Chinook helicopter to Bien Hoa which is near Saigon, then taking an air force jet transport from there to Hickam AFB. We still don't know what time we'll get there—probably about ten in the morning. I've got to go process now so I can be on the other end of the phone day after tomorrow. I need an anchor to keep both feet on the ground.
I love you.

On August 27, 1969, the last 300 9th Division troops,
having flown to Bien Hoa air base by helicopter,
aboard an air force transport for Hickam Field, Hawaii

CHAPTER 11: LAST MAN STANDING

Euphoria gave way to guarded happiness as GIs dressed in chemical suits boarded our Chinook when we landed at Bien Hoa air base. They said nothing while spraying us with what smelled like DDT. To this day, I do not know what it was. But I guess if you're coming straight from the teeming Mekong Delta to glorious Hawaii, they wanted to ensure no disease-carrying bugs were introduced into paradise by infested GIs.

As officers and NCOs, our work was far from finished, as we still had to herd the troops into their new barracks and begin the process of sorting them out once we landed at Hickam Field. That process became very difficult because all our personnel records were mistakenly placed on another flight that landed in Oakland, California, and were trucked to Fort Lewis, Washington. Fortunately, I had stuffed my computerized list into my bag, so we had some idea of our company rosters but really could not begin processing anyone until the records were flown to our location, which took a couple of days.

Compounding our challenge was the poor judgment of our CO, who directed me to give the troops passes to go off base once we landed. I warned him that about a third of my men had just been released from incarceration. Also, racial tensions simmering below the surface were beginning to bubble into view like lava rising from dormant volcanoes. As I recall, the first night was the worst. At about 10:00, I was rousted from a deep sleep I had postponed for at least a month to receive a call from the Honolulu Police Department. A frantic duty officer reported that my men were wrecking his city and his department was contemplating calling in the Hawaiian National Guard to quell what was on the verge of a riot.

I pleaded with him not to do that, and after hanging up I roamed Schofield Barracks, where we were billeted, grabbing any halfway sober NCO or officer and loading them into trucks. We armed ourselves with loaded .45s just in case and headed into Honolulu.

Somehow, we managed to corral the worst troublemakers, get them back to Schofield, and lock them in their barracks with guards at all the doors. Not too much damage had been done before the worst offenders were arrested and prepped for disciplinary action. The next day, when I went to Hickam Field to facilitate the return of our records, I noted that the huge "Welcome Back, 9th Division" banner that had been erected across one of the hangars was no longer there.

A few days later, Betsy arrived, and we settled into our very nice rented condo overlooking Makaha Beach and began the process of renewing our three-year-old marriage. Eventually, everyone in my battalion was sent to their next duty station or mustered out, leaving me the only soldier assigned to the 9th Signal Battalion, 9th Infantry—which created another military dilemma. Our unit had to be officially deactivated. In true army fashion, that meant a parade and ceremony, but a one-man parade I would not be. Rather, the 29th Hawaiian National Guard was issued 9th Division uniforms, medals and all, to stand in for the real thing that had long since melted into civilian or other military life.

Finally, one day, I signed the last official morning report, which listed only me before I changed the unit strength to zero.

Betsy and I attended a luncheon afterward, during which I had my first of several martinis. The ceremony that followed was impressive, with the Hawaiian Guardsmen, resplendent in our uniforms, marching in formation onto the Schofield Barracks Parade Field. Some general gave a speech I couldn't hear, my ears still ringing from the last artillery barrages leaving Dong Tam. The Hawaiian National Guard fired their howitzers in a final salute that sent many of us, on instinct, diving groundward. The ceremony concluded, and we gratefully repaired to the officers' club for more martinis, at which time I had my last unpleasant encounter with a senior officer.

A field-grade officer, whether colonel or general I cannot recall, approached me jovially and congratulated me for the great work I had done getting the battalion to Hawaii without losing a man. He then asked where my next station would be. Stifling the sarcasm and expletive I really wanted to retort with, I responded, "With all due respect, sir, I'm going home. My army career is over." I did an about-face and marched away, my now loose, over-the-collar hair no doubt making the officer think *Good riddance.*

The feeling was mutual.

EPILOGUE

Thanh Tran walked into my office that cold and cloudy day in mid-December fulfilling my hope for some excitement as I shuffled through the boring accreditation reports I was assembling into a persuasive document. But it wasn't excitement Thanh sought. His eyes betrayed a yearning for a friend, someone who would empathize with his story, someone who had experienced the war that uprooted his life, someone who cared about him. He had heard I was a Vietnam veteran and hoped I would be that person. After hearing his story, I immediately felt responsible for him, and we forged the kind of relationship we both needed—for him I was someone he could trust; for me he was Ho incarnate, someone else's child of war I could help.

When the war ended in 1975, Thanh Tran's father, a former ARVN officer, had been interred in a reeducation camp, where he died under torture, according to Thanh. His mother, a teacher, had been sentenced to in-country exile in a small village in the southern toe of Vietnam. Thanh became a "boat kid" sent to a camp near Hong Kong, where he was treated well but received no educational training while working for minimal wages.

Ultimately, Thanh reported, the political exiles were shipped to the United States, Thanh ended up in Everett, Massachusetts, and was fortunate not to be one of the "economic exiles" who were sent back to Vietnam. I never found out where Thanh lived or how he was supported as a teenager.

Thanh spoke fast and paced around my office as he described his dad, who served in the 7th ARVN Division, the sister unit to mine. Like many other South Vietnamese veterans, he had felt abandoned by the US. They believed the US gave too much to the North Vietnamese government to reach peace, tossing our former allies under the bus. It is possible that I might have met his Dad in my role as liaison to his unit. My heart sank at the thought that I had been part of what caused his father's death and the death of many others. Perhaps, by helping his son, I would, in a small way, be atoning for some of the sins committed during that time.

Thanh had not seen his mother in over a decade, and so I began the effort to raise the funds that would make the trip back to Vietnam possible. The trip to reunite Thanh with his family for a two-month visit would be expensive due to the bribes that would have to be paid in order to get through Vietnamese immigration and customs, as well as the cost of honoring Vietnamese culture. He not only would visit his mother and family in the deep Delta, he would also visit all of his relatives, especially the elder aunts and uncles in the more northern areas of Vietnam. When I asked why, he told me with great pride in his voice that in Vietnamese culture elders are deeply respected.

In a summer drizzle four months later, Thanh boarded a plane for Vietnam with cash taped to his legs under his trousers for the bribes required to process through Vietnamese immigration and customs. A small group of faculty and staff and I waved good-bye as his plane lifted off from Logan Airport in Boston. I feared for his safety, as I would my own children as they leave the security of my wing for the unknown. I wanted to be with him. I was grateful that his family would know a former ally who betrayed them was paying them back for the pain my country and I had caused.

Thanh arrived in Vietnam some twenty hours later, the twenty-three-year-old who had last seen his homeland at the age of eleven, peering out from under the tarp of an overloaded boat of refugees headed for Hong Kong.

He was not treated like the returning hero he saw himself as. The police ignored his entry permit and asked him "unreasonable questions." And so, after the bribes were paid, he met up with one of our contacts in Saigon and finally arrived safely at a relative's house nearby. A few days later he traveled to the village deep in the Delta where his mother lived and where he would begin again as a member of his loving family.

It would be a long journey for Thanh, as it has been for me, and in many ways still is. Both of us would try to reconcile all that had happened, and both of us would try to find a new way forward. Thanh would leave his family for a second time and return to the United States, broken-hearted and longing for his family but determined to build a life he could be proud of. Through life's many twists and turns, he did just that.

I look back on my life and the young man I was when I returned from a Daytona spring break in my senior year of college and interviewed for a job marketing gasoline. I never could have imagined then how signing up for ROTC in my sophomore year in order to gain the forty-dollar monthly stipend would lead me to my Vietnam experience and ultimately to a very different life. I promised myself that if I got out of Vietnam alive, I would spend my life in service to others through education and participating in the political process that got us into Vietnam in the first place.

I would like to be able to say that one day there will be no more Vietnams or orphans like Ho or families torn apart like Thanh's or all the families everywhere who grieve for their loved ones who never returned. I have no way of knowing what the world will evolve into. But I do know this: It's not too late for those who are now the age I was when I went to Vietnam to live lives that help the world find higher ground without going to war. We need not commit the errors of the past to achieve what I and my generation had to learn the hard way. My generation's claims to greatness rely on the next generation learning from, not repeating, the mistakes of the past. Otherwise what I and my generation endured will have truly been in vain.

Joyous reunion in Vietnam ends with sad return to U.S.

Following is SSC student Thanh Tran's account of his return to Vietnam, the home he had not seen since he was 12 years old, contained in a letter sent to those who had helped him realize his dream.

By THANH TRAN

This past June I went back to Vietnam for two months to visit my family.

I have been back studying at Salem State College for a few weeks already. But my mind, my soul, and my heart still is in Vietnam.

My trip feels like it happened yesterday. The day that I had all my family, all of my friends and relatives, whom I loved so much. However, today, at this moment, I have nothing at all. They're gone. None of their sweet voices rise around me anymore. I have become a lonely person in a silent Bowditch Room writing a suffered journal with a lot of bitter tears.

I reflect almost everything about my past journey to Vietnam. It makes me feel bad when I recall it, because how can I improve some injustices of Vietnamese Communist policies?

I remember very clearly, when I first got out of the exit gate of the Saigon airport, the Communist police gave me a hard time. They didn't let me go through and tried to ask me some unreasonable questions, the purpose of which was to get money from me. For example, I gave some of the Communist police my Vietnamese entry permit, but they still didn't let me go through that gate until I gave them some money.

After that bad moment, I met one man who was there to pick me up at the airport. His name was Hai Hoang. He was one of Mr. Preecha's translators who I knew from an employee at Salem State.

He took me to Mr. Preecha's house. I stayed there only two days and then hurried to leave in order to see my family, which was far away in the delta of South Vietnam. After spending ten hours on the bus, I finally got home. However, I had trouble figuring out where my house was located. How different it was! My town changed a lot.

The houses of my town were more crowded than I remembered. My brothers, and my sisters, were there waiting for me. I made a phone call from Saigon when I first arrived to let them know I was coming.

I became emotional and cried so much when I first saw my mother, and family. I called her, saying, "Mom, your son is back ... I love you so much, Mom!" She said the same thing. Then she embraced me and both of us were happy to cry.

My house became an emotional place because my sisters and my brothers all cried. It could be said that that day was the happiest day in my life.

The day that I arrived home many people came to my house. They asked a bunch of questions, so much that I could not answer all of them. Questions like: What are you doing in America? What does America look like? Are there any Vietnamese there? What kind of food do you eat over there? How do you like America so far? Are American people nice to you?

I tried to answer as best I could. By that day, different people in town kept asking me the same questions. I stayed with my family about 20 days, then I left them and went to visit my aunt, who lives in the middle of Vietnam. The reason for this was because she was the one who spent a lot of money to send me on the small boat to escape Vietnam to find freedom somewhere else. What she had done for me I would never forget it in my present life.

After that I went back to Saigon, and brought my mother and my brothers to visit some parts of Saigon. Then I went down to Minh Hai to say farewell to my brothers, sister, relatives and friends before I came back to America. This time I had a lot of warm tears from seeing them off. I went back to Saigon with my brothers and mother and stayed with them there for a little while.

Finally I had to leave them, with a fully broken heart. My visit to my family was becoming my memories. Now, I don't know whenever I will be able to go back again to see them, because my college is so far away.

I am feeling very sad, because I can't help my family have a better life. I know my country has changed a lot in recent times, however, all the jobs of companies are used for some people whose relatives work in the government only. I really don't know what will happen to my country in the future. However, it will be hard to believe that Vietnamese people will have enough jobs to work in the future.

I may not know well what the Vietnamese government is trying to do for the Vietnamese people. However, I do know well that I am appreciative to all the people who donated money and gave me a big chance to see my family. Once again, I would like to say thank you to all of you, all of the ladies and gentleman that made this trip home possible. May God bless you, your family and your friends, and may all of you have healthy and happy futures.

Thanh Tran and Wayne Burton

ACKNOWLEDGMENTS

Following my professional retirement, our daughter, Abigail Flores, knowing of my interest in writing my Vietnam story, urged me to take a course at the neighboring University of New Hampshire called Writing the War Experience: An Introduction to Creative Nonfiction. The instructor, Joshua Folmar, not only taught the class the basics of writing well, but he infused the class with his own experiences as an Iraq War veteran bolstered with related writings. Joshua urged me to undertake writing this book having read some of the essays I wrote in his class.

During this period I met Maria Lane when attending a writing workshop for veterans in Gloucester, Massachusetts. She was writing a book about her father, a Korean War veteran, from his letters home. We bonded over our common endeavors, and she became a great source of encouragement for me as I experienced the peaks and valleys of writing a book.

At Maria's suggestion, the following summer I attended a writing workshop at UMass Boston's Joiner Center for the Study of War and its Consequences having heard of their renowned faculty, especially Lady Borton. Lady had worked in Vietnam and lived among the Vietnamese through Quaker service during and after the war and wrote from an intimacy with them true to their voices. My writing and thinking up until then had been two-dimensional, the American and South Vietnamese perspectives. Through Lady Borton and her book, *After Sorrow: An American Among the Vietnamese*, I gained a vital third perspective, that of those with whom we were fighting, the nationalistic Viet Cong.

Determined to develop my story grounded in the truth of my experience as described in the 240 letters I had salvaged through many moves, I engaged the services of my former Executive Assistant, Jacqueline Sakamoto, to transcribe the letters from the typed copies into digital files, allowing me to analyze them with qualitative data analysis software called NVivo. I had used similar invaluable software to code and analyze the fifty in-depth interviews I had done with faculty when writing my doctoral dissertation at Vanderbilt on faculty culture. Jackie has a remarkable ability to accomplish with high quality detailed work. Over many, many hours she transformed my letters into a highly usable database.

Most valuable to me as I finally sat down to write the book was the help and enthusiasm of Claire Alemian, herself a new author who had penned her remarkable book, *In the Shadow of Light,* the year before.

What motivated me most, though, was my need to explain to our children, Jeffrey, Abigail, and Peter, how I got to be who I am. It is to them I am grateful, as well as their spouses, Jeffrey Flores and Jessica Burton, and our grandchildren, Jeffery and Colin Flores and Nora and Miles Burton, for this opportunity to offer my experience to guide them in the hopes it is not repeated.

ABOUT THE AUTHOR

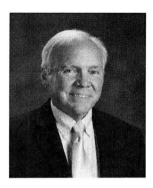

President Emeritus of North Shore Community College (NSCC), Wayne Myles Burton was raised in Belmont, Massachusetts. After graduating from Belmont High School, he was commissioned a second lieutenant in the US Army through the ROTC program at Bowdoin College, where he majored in economics.

Leaving the army after serving in Germany and Vietnam with the rank of captain, he received his MBA from the University of New Hampshire (UNH) and later earned his EdD in Higher Education Leadership from Vanderbilt University.

The author chaired the Salem Harbor Community Development Corporation while Dean of the School of Business at Salem State University and chaired the board of the North Shore Chamber of Commerce while serving as president of NSCC. Prior to both assignments he served sixteen years as Assistant Dean and Director of Accreditation for UNH's School of Business.

He served four terms (eight years) in the New Hampshire House of Representatives and currently is finishing his second term as a Town Councilor in Durham, New Hampshire. He and his wife, Betsy, continue to live in Durham as they have for almost fifty years. They have three children and four grandchildren.

While serving in Vietnam, the US Army awarded the author three Bronze Stars, two Army Commendation Medals, and a Meritorious Unit Commendation. The Republic of South Vietnam bestowed on him the Gallantry Cross with Palm, the Civic Action Honor medal, and the Signal Corps Badge.